VOLUME 5

OLD TEST

THE NEW COLLEGEVILLE BIBLE COMMENTARY

NUMBERS

Irene Nowell, O.S.B.

SERIES EDITOR

Daniel Durken, O.S.B.

LITURGICAL PRESS

Collegeville, Minnesota

www.litpress.org

Nihil obstat: Reverend Robert Harren, *Censor deputatus.*
Imprimatur: ✠ Most Reverend John F. Kinney, J.C.D., D.D., Bishop of St. Cloud, Minnesota, December 17, 2010.

Design by Ann Blattner.

1   2   3   4   5   6   7   8   9

Library of Congress Cataloging-in-Publication Data

Nowell, Irene, 1940–
        Numbers / Irene Nowell.
            p.   cm. — (The new Collegeville Bible commentary. Old Testament ; v. 5)
        ISBN 978-0-8146-2839-3
        1. Bible. O.T. Numbers—Commentaries.   I. Title.

        BS1265.53.N69   2010
        222'.1407—dc22   2009036629

CONTENTS

ABBREVIATIONS

Books of the Bible

Acts—Acts of the Apostles
Amos—Amos
Bar—Baruch
1 Chr—1 Chronicles
2 Chr—2 Chronicles
Col—Colossians
1 Cor—1 Corinthians
2 Cor—2 Corinthians
Dan—Daniel
Deut—Deuteronomy
Eccl (or Qoh)—Ecclesiastes
Eph—Ephesians
Esth—Esther
Exod—Exodus
Ezek—Ezekiel
Ezra—Ezra
Gal—Galatians
Gen—Genesis
Hab—Habakkuk
Hag—Haggai
Heb—Hebrews
Hos—Hosea
Isa—Isaiah
Jas—James
Jdt—Judith
Jer—Jeremiah
Job—Job
Joel—Joel
John—John
1 John—1 John
2 John—2 John
3 John—3 John
Jonah—Jonah
Josh—Joshua
Jude—Jude
Judg—Judges
1 Kgs—1 Kings

2 Kgs—2 Kings
Lam—Lamentations
Lev—Leviticus
Luke—Luke
1 Macc—1 Maccabees
2 Macc—2 Maccabees
Mal—Malachi
Mark—Mark
Matt—Matthew
Mic—Micah
Nah—Nahum
Neh—Nehemiah
Num—Numbers
Obad—Obadiah
1 Pet—1 Peter
2 Pet—2 Peter
Phil—Philippians
Phlm—Philemon
Prov—Proverbs
Ps(s)—Psalms
Rev—Revelation
Rom—Romans
Ruth—Ruth
1 Sam—1 Samuel
2 Sam—2 Samuel
Sir—Sirach
Song—Song of Songs
1 Thess—1 Thessalonians
2 Thess—2 Thessalonians
1 Tim—1 Timothy
2 Tim—2 Timothy
Titus—Titus
Tob—Tobit
Wis—Wisdom
Zech—Zechariah
Zeph—Zephaniah

The Book of Numbers

Title

The English title of this book is Numbers, a fitting name for a book that contains not only two censuses of the people (chs. 1 and 26) and a separate census of the Levites (ch. 3), but also many lists: the offerings of the tribes to the tabernacle (ch. 7); the measurements of grain, wine, and oil to accompany sacrifices (ch. 15); the designated sacrifices for all occasions (chs. 28–29); the stages of the wilderness journey (ch. 33); and the boundaries of the land (ch. 34). The Hebrew title of the book is *Bemidbar*, "in the wilderness," a word found in the first verse of the book, which aptly describes its contents.

Chronology and geography

Most of the stories in Numbers seem to be clustered around the first two years and the fortieth year after the exodus event. The book opens on the first day of the second month of the second year after the exodus from Egypt. The people have been encamped at Sinai almost a year, since the first day of the third month of the first year after the exodus (Exod 19:1). There is a flashback of a month in Numbers 7–9: The tribal leaders make their offerings when Moses completes the construction of the tabernacle, the first day of the *first* month of year two (Num 7:1; see Exod 40:2, 17). The Passover is celebrated in the same month, on the fourteenth day of the first month of year two (Num 9:1-5). The flashback ends and the chronology resumes with the people's departure from Sinai on the twentieth day of the second month of year two (Num 10:11).

Thus the events of Numbers 1:1–10:10 occur in the first twenty days of the second month of the second year after the exodus. Then there is a gap in the chronology. No dates are indicated until chapter 20 and the date that appears in that chapter is incomplete: The Israelites arrive at Kadesh in the wilderness of Zin in the first month; neither the day nor the year is mentioned (Num 20:1). A clue to the year may be found in the announcement of Aaron's death in 20:22-29. Elsewhere his death is reported to be on the first day of the fifth month of the fortieth year after the departure from Egypt (Num 33:38). No further dates appear in the book.

Figure 1: Chronology

First census (1:1)	Day 1	Month 2	Year 2
Tribal offerings (7:1; see Exod 40:2, 17)	*Day 1*	*Month 1*	*Year 2*
Passover (9:1-5)	*Day 14*	*Month 1*	*Year 2*
Departure from Sinai (10:11)	Day 20	Month 2	Year 2
Arrival at Kadesh (20:1)	---	Month 1	---
Aaron's death (20:22-29; 33:38)	Day 1	Month 5	Year 40

For the first several chapters the people are encamped at Mount Sinai (1:1–10:10). From there they travel to two otherwise unknown wilderness locations whose names recall the people's murmuring against the Lord: Taberah and Kibroth-hattaavah (11:3, 34-35). From there they travel to Hazeroth where Miriam and Aaron complain against Moses (11:35). These places seem to be in the southern part of the Sinai Peninsula.

Then the people turn north and come to the wilderness of Paran in the northeastern part of the Sinai Peninsula. From here Moses sends spies to scout out the land (13:3). A problem arises when the place is also named Kadesh (13:26). Apparently in one version of the wilderness story Israel arrived at Kadesh fairly soon after the departure from Egypt, since they are told in the wilderness of Paran that they will wander for forty years before entering the Promised Land (14:29-34). Another version of the story puts their arrival at Kadesh in what seems to be the fortieth year of their sojourn in the wilderness (20:1). Both traditions were preserved. Kadesh is located in the northern part of the wilderness of Paran, close to the wilderness of Zin. See map on page 154.

From Kadesh the people begin their approach to the Promised Land. They arrive at Mount Hor on the border of Edom where Aaron dies (20:22-27). They take the Red Sea road according to God's instructions (14:25), possibly going as far south as the Gulf of Aqaba (called the Red Sea in 21:4). They then go north to bypass Edom on the west, camping at two otherwise unknown sites, Oboth and Iye-abarim. From there they travel around Moab to the west, camping first at the Wadi Zered between Edom and Moab and arriving at the Wadi Arnon, which forms the northern border of Moab (21:11-13). The remaining sites are all in the plains of Moab. Mount Pisgah is, according to Deuteronomy, the site of Moses' death (Deut 34:1-6).

Figure 2: Itinerary (compare Numbers 33)

Mount Sinai	1:1–10:10
Wilderness: Taberah, Kibroth-hattaavah, Hazeroth	10:11–12:15
Wilderness of Paran (at Kadesh?)	12:16; 13:3 13:26
Wilderness of Zin (Kadesh/Meribah)	20:1, 13, 14, 16, 22
Mount Hor on the border of Edom	20:22-27
The Red Sea road	21:4; see 14:25
Oboth and Iye-abarim across from Moab	21:11
Wadi Zered	21:12
Wadi Arnon north of Moab	21:13
To the plains of Moab: Beer, Mattanah, Nahaliel, Bamoth, Pisgah Shittim/Peor in the plains of Moab	21:17-20 25:1, 3

Structure

The basic structure of the book is set by the censuses of two generations and the primary stages of the itinerary: (1) preparation for the departure from Sinai (1:1–10:10); (2) forty-year wandering of the exodus generation from Sinai to the plains of Moab (10:11–25:18); (3) a new generation on the plains of Moab (26:1–36:13).

Another important characteristic of the structure of the book is the interweaving of narrative and law. After chapters 1–10, which consist mostly of legislative and organizational material, stories set the stage for laws. Stories of murmuring and rebellion (chs. 11–14) lead to the legislation concerning sacrifices and sin offerings (ch. 15). Korah's challenge that all the people of God are holy and should be allowed to handle holy things (ch. 16) is followed by the legislation concerning priests and Levites (chs. 17–18) and preparation of purification water (ch. 19).

Even as the murmuring continues, the report of the deaths of Miriam and Aaron (ch. 20) introduces the last leg of the journey toward the Promised Land (ch. 21). The oracles of Balaam show Israel as blessed by God (chs. 22–24), but the incident at Baal-Peor reveals their weakness (ch. 25). In chapter 26 a new generation is introduced and counted. The rest of the book is filled with legislation for this new generation in the Promised Land: inheritance and allotment of the land (chs. 27, 32, 34, 36), observance of festivals (ch. 29), validity of vows (ch. 30), and cities of asylum (ch. 35). Even this collection of laws, however, is interrupted by narrative, the battle against the Midianites (ch. 31); this story provides the model for waging Holy War. Chapter 33 is a summary of the stages on the journey.

Sources

For almost two centuries the Documentary Hypothesis was considered the best way to analyze the sources in the pentateuchal (first five books of the Old Testament) narrative. According to this theory there were four major sources that threaded their way through the narrative from creation to the entrance into the land: Yahwist (tenth-century Judah); Elohist (ninth-century Israel); Deuteronomist (seventh-century Jerusalem); Priestly (sixth-century Babylon). According to the theory, these sources, each a written version based on oral tradition and the situation of the intended audience, were finally compiled in the sixth-century Babylonian exile to form the final edition of the Pentateuch. It has become increasingly clear, however, how difficult it is to follow any one of these sources throughout the Pentateuch. So different models are being proposed to assist the reader in understanding the contradictions, duplicate stories, and different styles that appear in these books, sometimes in close proximity to each other.

The assumption in this commentary is that various traditions are represented in the book of Numbers. One tradition is interested in matters of worship and law, and is probably also responsible for the various censuses and lists. This tradition will be called "Priestly." Other traditions supply some of the murmuring stories and a variant report of the itinerary of the wilderness wandering. These traditions will be called collectively "pre-Priestly." No attempt is made to date any of these traditional sources.

Content

The Hebrew title of the book indicates one of its major themes: the wilderness. The wilderness (or desert) is both a positive and a negative symbol in the Old Testament. It is a place of constant murmuring and rebellion (e.g., Exod 15:22–17:7; Num 11–14), but it is also the place of Israel's "honeymoon" with God, the place where they were totally dependent on God who provided for them abundantly (e.g., Jer 2:1-3; Hos 2:16-17). Both connotations often appear together (see Num 20:2-13; Deut 8:1-5). It is in the wilderness where those who were slaves in Egypt make covenant with God and become God's people (Exod 19:1-8). The book of Numbers describes their testing in the wilderness and the implications of being God's covenant people.

A significant implication of being God's people is that God chooses to live in their midst, literally to pitch a tent with them. The "tent of meeting" is mentioned almost sixty times in the book of Numbers. In this book the tent is ordinarily understood to be in the center of the camp (2:17; 3:38). The tribes encamp on all four sides of it with the Levites, as guardians of the tent, encamped between the other tribes and the tent itself (chs. 2–3; see Figure 4, p. 17). Careful instructions are given for the dismantling of the tent and its transport in the midst of the line of march (4:1-33).

The ark of the covenant is inside the tent (3:31; 4:5) and sacrificial worship is offered at the tent (6:18). God speaks to Moses at the tent, makes decisions and gives instructions (see 7:89; 17:7-8, 19). The sacred place in the midst of the camp is also called the tabernacle (Hebrew *mishkan*; e.g., 1:50, 51, 53) and the sanctuary (Hebrew *miqdash* or *qodesh*; e.g., 3:28, 31, 38). God's presence in the tent is the reason for the purity laws in chapters 1–10. The holy God lives in their midst. Thus they must be a holy people.

An alternate tradition (pre-Priestly) places the tent outside the camp (11:24-27; 12:4-5). According to this tradition God speaks to anyone who comes to this tent (Exod 33:7), but sacrifice is not offered here and the ark is separate from the tent (10:33-35; 14:44).

The Levites are set apart throughout the book of Numbers. They are given the responsibility to care for the tent: to guard it (1:47-53), transport it (3:21-38; 4:1-33), and to assist the priests who minister before it (3:6-10). They camp between the tent and the rest of the people in order both to protect the sanctuary and to protect the people from straying too close to the holy place. They are also designated as substitutes for the firstborn sons who are God's own possession (3:5-13, 40-51).

The goal of Israel's journey through the wilderness is the Promised Land. In traveling toward this land and taking possession of it, they will need to do battle against the native populations. God instructs them to do battle in a certain way, which has been paradoxically called "Holy War." First of all, they must always recognize that it is God who gives the victory; they do not win by their own power. At the beginning of their journey the song of the ark indicates God's leadership: "Arise, O LORD, may your enemies be scattered" (10:35). They forget this principle in an unsuccessful attack against the Amalekites and Canaanites (14:39-45). When other peoples attack them, however, they remember God's power and are successful (21:1-3, 21-35).

Second, they must not go to war for gain; they must dedicate all the spoils to God. This dedication is sometimes called the "ban" and the spoils as "doomed" (Hebrew *herem*). Carrying out the *herem* happens in two ways: If the defeated people are not inhabitants of the Promised Land, all or some of the spoils may be given to the sanctuary both through sacrifice and for the support of the priests and Levites (18:14; 31:9-12, 25-47; see Deut 20:10-15). If the defeated people are one of the five Canaanite groups, everything may be destroyed and all the people killed (21:1-3). The reason for the distinction is that the native Canaanites may lead the Israelites into worship of other gods (see Deut 20:16-18).

Reading the book of Numbers

The book of Numbers rarely makes the top ten list of favorite biblical books. But there are several insights regarding how to live as God's people that can be gained from a thoughtful reading of this book. First, it is true for us also that the holy God lives in our midst. How then should we act? What kind of people should we be? Second, we too are a people on the way. We too journey through the wilderness; we too grumble when we do not get what we want. It is vital to remember that the living God supplies all our needs with care and generosity. Third, God chooses people to lead us on our journey. How can we learn to trust those leaders and to trust God who chooses them?

Fourth, we too have enemies who would prevent us from entering into the land God has promised us, most notably our own sinfulness. We must realize that we do not conquer evil by our own strength but only through God's power. We are called to sing God's praise, dedicating everything that has been given us back to our generous God. Finally, although the message is serious, several of the stories in Numbers are humorous. It is a gift to recognize God's gentle humor in our own lives.

The Book of Numbers

I. Census and Preparation for the Departure from Sinai

1 The Census. ¹In the second year after the Israelites' departure from the land of Egypt, on the first day of the second month, the LORD said to Moses at the tent of meeting in the wilderness of Sinai: ²Take a census of the whole community of the Israelites, by clans and ancestral houses, registering by name each male individually. ³You and Aaron shall enroll in companies all the men in Israel of twenty years or more who are fit for military service.

CENSUS AND PREPARATION FOR THE DEPARTURE FROM SINAI

Numbers 1:1–10:10

1:1-3 The census

The book of Numbers begins with a numbering, a census of all the men able to fight. The opening sentence is typical of the Priestly source of the Pentateuch (see introduction): identifying everything that happens as a direct command of the Lord to Moses and setting the stage by giving the date and the place of what follows.

God orders the census taking on the first day of the second month in the second year after the departure from Egypt. The exodus is the central event for Israel just as the life, death, and resurrection of Jesus Christ is the central event for Christians. Just as Christians set the beginning of their calendar by Christ, marking all the years as *Anno Domini* (Year of the Lord), so here Israel dates these happenings as if time began with the exodus. The community has been at Sinai since the third month of the first year after the exodus (Exod 19:1). In less than a month they will depart on the twentieth day of this second month of year two (Num 10:11). It is time to make final preparations.

Mount Sinai is the place of covenant making. God has been revealed to them in a great theophany (manifestation), given them the law, and sealed the covenant, promising to make them a chosen people, a priestly

Moses' Assistants. ⁴With you there shall be a man from each tribe, each the head of his ancestral house. ⁵These are the names of those who are to assist you:

from Reuben: Elizur, son of Shedeur;
⁶from Simeon: Shelumiel, son of Zurishaddai;
⁷from Judah: Nahshon, son of Amminadab;
⁸from Issachar: Nethanel, son of Zuar;
⁹from Zebulun: Eliab, son of Helon;
¹⁰for the descendants of Joseph: from Ephraim: Elishama, son of Ammihud; and from Manasseh: Gamaliel, son of Pedahzur;
¹¹from Benjamin: Abidan, son of Gideoni;
¹²from Dan: Ahiezer, son of Ammishaddai;
¹³from Asher: Pagiel, son of Ochran;
¹⁴from Gad: Eliasaph, son of Reuel;
¹⁵from Naphtali: Ahira, son of Enan.

¹⁶These were the elect of the community, leaders of their ancestral tribes,

---

kingdom, and a holy nation (Exod 19–24). God has given them instructions for building the tabernacle as a divine dwelling place (Exod 25–31; 35–40). They have already broken the covenant and God has renewed it (Exod 32–34). Now they must get ready to go on through the wilderness toward the Promised Land.

The Lord orders Moses to take a census of the whole community. The specific terms used to identify these people indicate two important realities: They are a worshiping community (the *ʿedah*) and they are bound together by familial ties (the "house of the father" or "ancestral house," and the "clan" or extended family). The persons to be numbered, however, are only the men over twenty years old who are thus eligible for military service. Moses and Aaron are to take a head count (literally, "by the skull") and register each eligible male by name. They will not only be numbered, but they will be assigned to military divisions or "companies."

1:4-19 Moses' assistants

Moses and Aaron do not have to take this census alone. They are to enlist the assistance of a leader from each of the twelve tribes. The assistants are named, tribe by tribe. First, the tribes from Leah's own sons are named in birth order: Reuben, Simeon, Judah, Issachar, Zebulun. Then the tribes named for Rachel's two sons are listed: Joseph (represented by his sons, Ephraim and Manasseh) and Benjamin. Finally, the tribes representing the four sons of the maids, Bilhah and Zilpah, are named in no apparent order: Dan, Asher, Gad, and Naphtali (see Gen 29:31–30:24). Since the tribe of Levi is omitted (see 1:47-54), the tribe of Joseph is divided between Ephraim and Manasseh (Joseph's two sons) in order to fill out the number twelve.

heads of the clans of Israel. [17]So Moses and Aaron took these men who had been designated by name, [18]and assembled the whole community on the first day of the second month. Every man of twenty years or more then registered individually his name and lineage according to clan and ancestral house, [19]as the LORD had commanded Moses. So he enrolled them in the wilderness of Sinai.

Count of the Twelve Tribes. [20]Of the descendants of Reuben, the firstborn of Israel, registered individually by name and lineage according to their clans and ancestral houses, every male of twenty years or more, everyone fit for military service: [21]those enrolled from the tribe of Reuben were forty-six thousand five hundred.

[22]Of the descendants of Simeon, registered individually by name and lineage according to their clans and ancestral houses, every male of twenty years or more, everyone fit for military service: [23]those enrolled from the tribe of Simeon were fifty-nine thousand three hundred.

[24]Of the descendants of Gad, registered by name and lineage according to their clans and ancestral houses, every male of twenty years or more, everyone fit for military service: [25]those enrolled from the tribe of Gad were forty-five thousand six hundred and fifty.

[26]Of the descendants of Judah, registered by name and lineage according to their clans and ancestral houses, every male of twenty years or more, everyone fit for military service: [27]those enrolled from the tribe of Judah were seventy-four thousand six hundred.

[28]Of the descendants of Issachar, registered by name and lineage according to their clans and ancestral houses, every male of twenty years or more, everyone fit for military service: [29]those enrolled

---

With the exception of Nahshon, son of Amminadab of the tribe of Judah (Exod 6:23), the individual representatives of each tribe appear only here and in chapters 2, 7, and 10. Many of their names, however, are based on the divine names El and Shaddai: for example, Elizur, "my God is rock"; Shedeur, "the Almighty gives light"; Shelumiel, "God is my peace"; Zurishaddai, "the Almighty is my rock." None, however, are based on the sacred name, Yahweh. After the assistants are named, Moses and Aaron carry out God's instructions exactly.

1:20-46 Count of the twelve tribes

The results of the census are reported tribe by tribe. The same formula is repeated for each tribe. Only the first two tribes have some different phrases. Reuben is identified as the firstborn (1:20). Those registered for Reuben and Simeon are identified as males who are counted "individually" (literally, "by head" or "polled"). The order of the tribes is similar to the order in the list of assistants. The only exception is the tribe of Gad, which is inserted between Simeon and Judah.

from the tribe of Issachar were fifty-four thousand four hundred.

30Of the descendants of Zebulun, registered by name and lineage according to their clans and ancestral houses, every male of twenty years or more, everyone fit for military service: 31those enrolled from the tribe of Zebulun were fifty-seven thousand four hundred.

32Of the descendants of Joseph:

Of the descendants of Ephraim, registered by name and lineage according to their clans and ancestral houses, every male of twenty years or more, everyone fit for military service: 33those enrolled from the tribe of Ephraim were forty thousand five hundred.

34Of the descendants of Manasseh, registered by name and lineage according to their clans and ancestral houses, every male of twenty years or more, ev-

eryone fit for military service: 35those enrolled from the tribe of Manasseh were thirty-two thousand two hundred.

36Of the descendants of Benjamin, registered by name and lineage according to their clans and ancestral houses, every male of twenty years or more, everyone fit for military service: 37those enrolled from the tribe of Benjamin were thirty-five thousand four hundred.

38Of the descendants of Dan, registered by name and lineage according to their clans and ancestral houses, every male of twenty years or more, everyone fit for military service: 39those enrolled from the tribe of Dan were sixty-two thousand seven hundred.

40Of the descendants of Asher, registered by name and lineage according to their clans and ancestral houses, every

Figure 3: Listing of Tribes

Genesis 29–30 *Birth Order*	Genesis 46 *To Egypt*	Genesis 49 *Blessing*	Numbers 1 *1st Census*	Numbers 2, 7, 10 *Order of March*
Reuben	Reuben	Reuben	Reuben	Judah
Simeon	Simeon	Simeon	Simeon	Issachar
Levi	Levi	Levi	Gad	Zebulun
Judah	Judah	Judah	Judah	Reuben
Dan	Issachar	Zebulun	Issachar	Simeon
Naphtali	Zebulun	Issachar	Zebulun	Gad
Gad	Gad	Dan	Ephraim	Ephraim
Asher	Asher	Gad	Manasseh	Manasseh
Issachar	Joseph	Asher	Benjamin	Benjamin
Zebulun	Benjamin	Naphtali	Dan	Dan
Joseph	Dan	Joseph	Asher	Asher
Benjamin	Naphtali	Benjamin	Naphtali	Naphtali

male of twenty years or more, everyone fit for military service: ⁴¹those enrolled from the tribe of Asher were forty-one thousand five hundred.

⁴²Of the descendants of Naphtali, registered by name and lineage according to their clans and ancestral houses, every male of twenty years or more, everyone fit for military service: ⁴³those enrolled from the tribe of Naphtali were fifty-three thousand four hundred.

⁴⁴It was these who were enrolled, each according to his ancestral house, by Moses and Aaron and the twelve leaders of Israel. ⁴⁵The total enrollment of the Israelites of twenty years or more, according to their ancestral houses, everyone fit for military service in Israel—⁴⁶the total enrollment was six hundred and three thousand, five hundred and fifty.

Levites Omitted in the Census. ⁴⁷Now the Levites were not enrolled by

---

The total number of men eligible for military service registered from the twelve tribes is 603,550. The number is unrealistic. If there were 600,000 able men among the Israelites at Sinai, the whole people, including women and children, would have numbered around two million. The Sinai desert could not have supported a group that size. Thus the number must have another meaning. First of all, the large number indicates that Israel need not fear anyone who resists its entrance into the Promised Land. Second, the same number of men were assessed the half-shekel sanctuary tax. That tax payment covered the exact cost of the pedestals for the sanctuary along with the veil and the hooks and silver-plating for the columns (Exod 38:26-28).

Third, the number may have symbolic value. In ancient Israel the same symbols were used for letters and numbers (analogous to the use of letters for numbers in Roman numerals). Thus the symbol for the first letter of the alphabet was also used for the number one; the symbol for the second letter served also as the number two, and so on. If the letters for *bene-yisraʾel* ("sons of Israel" = Israelites) are added up, they equal 603. So 603,000 would be the Israelites times a thousand. Finally, since Babylonian mathematics worked from a base of sixty and the Priestly source for this section of Numbers was probably completed during the Babylonian exile, it is not surprising to find a number close to 600,000.

1:47-54 Levites omitted in the census

The Levites are not included in the census because they have other duties. They are not expected to take up arms. Rather they are responsible for the tabernacle and everything that belongs to it. They put it up, take it down, and carry it whenever it is moved. They are responsible to guard it and to perform the liturgical services. Any other person who approaches

◄ their ancestral tribe with the others. ⁴⁸For the LORD had told Moses, ⁴⁹The tribe of Levi alone you shall not enroll nor include in the census along with the other Israelites. ⁵⁰You are to give the Levites charge of the tabernacle of the covenant with all its equipment and all that belongs to it. It is they who shall carry the tabernacle with all its equipment and who shall be its ministers; and they shall camp all around the tabernacle. ⁵¹When the tabernacle is to move on, the Levites shall take it down; when the tabernacle is to be pitched, it is the Levites who shall set it up. Any unauthorized person who comes near it shall be put to death. ⁵²The other Israelites shall camp according to their companies, each in their own divisional camps, ⁵³but the Levites shall camp around the tabernacle of the cove-

nant to ensure that God's wrath will not fall upon the Israelite community. The Levites shall keep guard over the tabernacle of the covenant. ⁵⁴The Israelites complied; they did just as the LORD had commanded Moses.

Arrangement of the Tribes. ¹The LORD said to Moses and Aaron: ²The Israelites shall camp, each in their own divisions, under the ensigns of their ancestral houses. They shall camp at some distance all around the tent of meeting.

³Encamped on the east side, toward the sunrise, shall be the divisional camp of Judah, arranged in companies. The leader of the Judahites is Nahshon, son of Amminadab, ⁴and the enrollment of his company is seventy-four thousand six hundred. ⁵Encamped beside it is the tribe of Issachar. The leader of the Issa-

---

this sacred tabernacle is subject to the death penalty. A census of the Levites will be taken in Numbers 3.

The chapter closes with the notice that God's command to Moses (v. 1) had been fulfilled exactly.

2:1-34 Arrangement of the tribes

The Lord issues a new command to Moses (see 1:1 ["said"], 1:19 and 54 ["commanded"], 1:48 ["told"]). This command has to do with the arrangement of the tribes in their encampment and the placement of the tent of meeting (see introduction: tent of meeting). The twelve tribes, minus Levi who is replaced by the division of Joseph into the tribes of Ephraim and Manasseh, are set up in groups of three tribes each on the four sides of the tent of meeting. The tribal leaders identified in 1:5-15 are named again and the census count from 1:20-42 is repeated. A major tribe leads each of the four tribal divisions: Judah on the east, Reuben on the south, Ephraim on the west, and Dan on the north.

► This symbol indicates a cross-reference number in the *Catechism of the Catholic Church*. See page 152 for number citations.

charites is Nethanel, son of Zuar, [6]and the enrollment of his company is fifty-four thousand four hundred. [7]Also the tribe of Zebulun. The leader of the Zebulunites is Eliab, son of Helon, [8]and the enrollment of his company is fifty-seven thousand four hundred. [9]The total enrollment of the camp of Judah by companies is one hundred and eighty-six thousand four hundred. They shall be first on the march.

[10]The divisional camp of Reuben shall be on the south side, by companies. The leader of the Reubenites is Elizur, son of Shedeur, [11]and the enrollment of his company is forty-six thousand five hundred. [12]Encamped beside it is the tribe of Simeon. The leader of the Simeonites is Shelumiel, son of Zurishaddai, [13]and the enrollment of his company is fifty-nine thousand three hundred.

[14]Next is the tribe of Gad. The leader of the Gadites is Eliasaph, son of Reuel, [15]and the enrollment of his company is forty-five thousand six hundred and fifty. [16]The total enrollment of the camp of Reuben by companies is one hundred and fifty-one thousand four hundred and fifty. They shall be second on the march.

[17]Then the tent of meeting and the camp of the Levites shall set out in the midst of the divisions. As they camp, so also they will march, each in place, by their divisions.

[18]The divisional camp of Ephraim shall be on the west side, by companies. The leader of the Ephraimites is Elishama, son of Ammihud, [19]and the enrollment of his company is forty thousand five hundred. [20]Beside it shall be the tribe of Manasseh. The leader of

Figure 4: Arrangement of Tribes around the Tent of Meeting

	Asher	DAN	Naphtali	
Benjamin		*Merari*		Issachar
EPHRAIM	*Gershonites*	TENT OF MEETING	*Moses with Aaron & his sons*	JUDAH
Manasseh		*Kohathites*		Zebulun
	Gad	REUBEN	Simeon	

The listing of the tribes is not in the same order as chapter 1 (see Figure 3, p. 14). Nor is it related to the geographical locations of the tribal settlements in Israel. It seems rather to be by later importance. Judah, the tribe favored in Jacob's farewell address (Gen 49) and the ancestor of David, holds the prime location: the east at the entrance to the tent of meeting. Reuben, the firstborn, follows at the south. Ephraim, the primary tribe of the northern kingdom, Israel, is next at the west. Dan, a tribe that did in fact move to the north and fell to the Assyrians in Tiglath-Pileser's invasion during the eighth century, is last.

the Manassites is Gamaliel, son of Pedahzur, [21]and the enrollment of his company is thirty-two thousand two hundred. [22]Also the tribe of Benjamin. The leader of the Benjaminites is Abidan, son of Gideoni, [23]and the enrollment of his company is thirty-five thousand four hundred. [24]The total enrollment of the camp of Ephraim by companies is one hundred and eight thousand one hundred. They shall be third on the march.

[25]The divisional camp of Dan shall be on the north side, by companies. The leader of the Danites is Ahiezer, son of Ammishaddai, [26]and the enrollment of his company is sixty-two thousand seven hundred. [27]Encamped beside it shall be the tribe of Asher. The leader of the Asherites is Pagiel, son of Ochran, [28]and the enrollment of his company is forty-one thousand five hundred. [29]Also the tribe of Naphtali. The leader of the Naphtalites is Ahira, son of Enan, [30]and the enrollment of his company is fifty-three thousand four hundred. [31]The total enrollment of the camp of Dan is one hundred and fifty-seven thousand six hundred. They shall be the last on the march, by divisions.

[32]These are the enrollments of the Israelites according to their ancestral houses. The total enrollment of the camps by companies is six hundred and three thousand five hundred and fifty. [33]The Levites, however, were not enrolled with the other Israelites, just as the LORD had commanded Moses. [34]The Israelites did just as the LORD had commanded Moses; both in camp and on the march they were in their own divisions, everyone by clan and according to ancestral house.

3 The Sons of Aaron. [1]These are the offspring of Aaron and Moses at the time the LORD spoke to Moses on Mount Sinai. [2]These are the names of Aaron's

---

This order represents not only their encampment but also their order of march. The census was taken for military purposes and the arrangement of the tribes sets the order of military divisions. In this order the tribes will leave Sinai in chapter 10 and march toward the Promised Land. After chapter 10 the order of march is never again mentioned.

The Levites are again singled out. Their position in the midst of the camp and the midst of the line of march is stated at the exact center of the chapter, verse 17. More detail regarding their arrangement will be found in 3:21-39.

The chapter ends with two statements indicating the fulfillment of God's commands. The Levites were treated specially "just as the LORD had commanded Moses" and the tribal divisions, both in the camp and on the march, were arranged "just as the LORD had commanded Moses" (2:33-34).

3:1-4 The sons of Aaron

Now that the other tribes have been counted and put in order, chapters 3–4 turn to focus on the Levites: their genealogy, their special status as

sons: Nadab, the firstborn, Abihu, Eleazar, and Ithamar. ³These are the names of Aaron's sons, the anointed priests whom he ordained to serve as priests. ⁴But Nadab and Abihu died in the presence of the LORD when they offered unauthorized fire before the LORD in the wilderness of Sinai; and they left no sons. So only Eleazar and Ithamar served as priests during the lifetime of their father Aaron.

Levites in Place of the Firstborn.
⁵Now the LORD said to Moses: ⁶Summon the tribe of Levi and station them before Aaron the priest to serve him. ⁷They shall discharge his obligations and those of the whole community before the tent of meeting by maintaining the tabernacle. ⁸They shall have responsibility for all the furnishings of the tent of meeting and discharge the obligations of the Israelites by maintaining the tabernacle. ⁹You shall assign the Levites to Aaron and his sons; they have been assigned unconditionally to him from among the Israelites. ¹⁰But you will appoint only Aaron and his descendants to exercise the priesthood. Any unauthorized person who comes near shall be put to death.

¹¹The LORD said to Moses: ¹²I hereby take the Levites from the Israelites in place of every firstborn that opens the womb among the Israelites. The Levites, therefore, are mine, ¹³because every firstborn is mine. When I struck down all the firstborn in the land of Egypt, I consecrated to me every firstborn in Israel, human being and beast alike. They belong to me; I am the LORD.

substitutes for the firstborn, their census, their order of service and march, and their duties. The genealogy of Aaron, ancestor of the priests, sets the stage. (Moses' sons are not mentioned.)

Nadab and Abihu died after they offered "unauthorized fire" (Lev 10:1-7; 16:1-2) perhaps an unapproved kind of incense (see Exod 30:9). So the priestly descent continues only through Aaron's sons Eleazar and Ithamar. A description of their anointing as priests is found in Exodus 40:12-16.

3:5-13 Levites in place of the firstborn

The special status of the Levites is now explained: they are substitutes for the firstborn. After the tenth plague, when the Egyptian firstborn were killed but the Israelite firstborn were spared by the blood of the lamb, the Lord claimed for himself every firstborn male (Exod 13:2, 11-16). Every firstborn son must be given to the Lord, even those born in the wilderness. Since human sacrifice is not allowed among the Israelites, these firstborn must be redeemed in another way. The Levites stand in as substitutes, consecrated to the Lord. Their service redeems the firstborn. They are not priests, but are subordinate to them, assigned to serve them and to care for the tent of meeting and the tabernacle.

Census of the Levites. ¹⁴The LORD said to Moses in the wilderness of Sinai: ¹⁵Enroll the Levites by their ancestral houses and clans, enrolling every male of a month or more. ¹⁶Moses, therefore, enrolled them at the direction of the LORD, just as the LORD had charged.

¹⁷These were the sons of Levi by name: Gershon, Kohath and Merari. ¹⁸These were the names of the sons of Gershon, by their clans: Libni and Shimei. ¹⁹The sons of Kohath, by their clans, were Amram, Izhar, Hebron and Uzziel. ²⁰The sons of Merari, by their clans, were Mahli and Mushi. These were the clans of the Levites by their ancestral houses.

Duties of the Levitical Clans. ²¹To Gershon belonged the clan of the Libnites and the clan of the Shimeites; these were the clans of the Gershonites. ²²Their enrollment, registering every male of a month or more, was seven thousand five hundred. ²³The clans of the Gershonites

---

3:14-39 Census of the Levites and duties of the Levitical clans

The census of the other tribes was taken for military purposes; the census of the Levites is taken in order to determine how many firstborn are redeemed by their service. In the previous census only men over twenty years old were counted; this census includes all male Levites one month old or more. Even the infants can be substitutes for the firstborn. Infants younger than one month are not included since only after a month was an infant considered likely to survive. Just as the others were counted by tribes, each with a tribal leader, and were assigned places to camp and an order for the march, so also the Levites are counted by ancestral houses, each with a leader, and were given a specific place in the inner circle of the camp around the tent of meeting (see Figure 4, p. 17).

In addition, each ancestral house is given a specific responsibility in service of the tent of meeting. The Gershonites care for the hanging materials: the tent and its two-layer covering, the curtains and other hangings, and the necessary ropes for these materials (see introduction, "tent of meeting," pp. 8–9). The Kohathites were responsible for what was inside the sanctuary: the ark, table, menorah, altars, and utensils. Since Aaron is descended from this ancestral house, his son, the priest Eleazar, is named here. He has authority over the other three Levitical leaders and over all those who minister in the sanctuary. The third ancestral house, the Merarites, was given responsibility to care for and transport all the supports of the structure: the boards, bars, columns, pedestals, fittings, pegs, and ropes. Finally, Moses with Aaron and his sons encamped in the favored spot to the east in front of the entrance of the tent of meeting. Presumably they are numbered with the Kohathites.

camped behind the tabernacle, to the west. ²⁴The leader of the ancestral house of the Gershonites was Eliasaph, son of Lael. ²⁵At the tent of meeting their responsibility was the tabernacle: the tent and its covering, the curtain at the entrance of the tent of meeting, ²⁶the hangings of the court, the curtain at the entrance of the court enclosing both the tabernacle and the altar, and the ropes—whatever pertained to their maintenance.

²⁷To Kohath belonged the clans of the Amramites, the Izharites, the Hebronites, and the Uzzielites; these were the clans of the Kohathites. ²⁸Their enrollment, registering every male of a month or more, was eight thousand three hundred. They were the ones who performed the duties of the sanctuary. ²⁹The clans of the Kohathites camped on the south side of the tabernacle. ³⁰And the leader of their ancestral house of the clan of the Kohathites was Elizaphan, son of Uzziel. ³¹Their responsibility was the ark, the table, the menorah, the altars, the utensils of the sanctuary with which the priests minister, the veil, and everything pertaining to their maintenance. ³²The chief of the leaders of the Levites, however, was Eleazar, son of Aaron the priest; he was in charge of those who performed the duties of the sanctuary.

³³To Merari belonged the clans of the Mahlites and the Mushites; these were the clans of Merari. ³⁴Their enrollment, registering every male of a month or more, was six thousand two hundred. ³⁵The leader of the ancestral house of the clans of Merari was Zuriel, son of Abihail. They camped at the north side of the tabernacle. ³⁶The Merarites were assigned responsibility for the boards of the tabernacle, its bars, columns, pedestals, and all its fittings—and everything pertaining to their maintenance, ³⁷as well as the columns of the surrounding court with their pedestals, pegs and ropes.

³⁸East of the tabernacle, that is, in front of the tent of meeting, toward the sunrise, were camped Moses and Aaron and the latter's sons, performing the duties of the sanctuary incumbent upon the Israelites. Any unauthorized person who came near was to be put to death.

³⁹The total enrollment of the Levites whom Moses and Aaron enrolled at the direction of the LORD, by clans, every male a month old or more, was twenty-two thousand.

Census and Ransom of Firstborn. ⁴⁰The LORD then said to Moses: Enroll every firstborn male of the Israelites a month old or more, and count the number of their names. ⁴¹Then take the

3:40-51 Census and ransom of firstborn

The purpose of the census is stated again: the Levites are substitutes for all the firstborn. But the number is short. There are 22,273 firstborn males among the Israelites and only 22,000 Levites. So a new principle for redemption is established. The remaining 273 firstborn may be redeemed with money collected from the Israelites and paid to the priests (see Num 18:16). In this passage the cattle of the Levites also are designated as substitutes for the cattle of the rest of the Israelites here; however, the usual practice with

Levites for me—I am the LORD—in place of all the firstborn of the Israelites, as well as the Levites' cattle, in place of all the firstborn among the cattle of the Israelites. ⁴²So Moses enrolled all the firstborn of the Israelites, as the LORD had commanded him. ⁴³All the firstborn males, registered by name, of a month or more, numbered twenty-two thousand two hundred and seventy-three.

⁴⁴The LORD said to Moses: ⁴⁵Take the Levites in place of all the firstborn of the Israelites, and the Levites' cattle in place of their cattle, that the Levites may belong to me. I am the LORD. ⁴⁶As a redemption-price for the two hundred and seventy-three firstborn of the Israelites over and above the number of the Levites, ⁴⁷you shall take five shekels for each individual, according to the sanctuary shekel, twenty gerahs to the shekel. ⁴⁸Give this money to Aaron and his sons as a redemption-price for the extra number. ⁴⁹So Moses took the redemption money for those over and above the ones redeemed by the Levites. ⁵⁰From the firstborn of the Israelites he took the money, one thousand three hundred and sixty-five shekels according to the sanctuary shekel. ⁵¹He then gave this redemption money to Aaron and his sons, at the direction of the LORD, just as the LORD had commanded Moses.

4 Duties Further Defined. ¹The LORD said to Moses and Aaron: ²Take a census among the Levites of the Kohathites, by clans and ancestral houses, ³all between thirty and fifty years of age, who will join the personnel for doing tasks in the tent of meeting.

---

regard to domestic animals of the other tribes is that the firstborn males must be sacrificed (see Num 18:17-18).

4:1-33 Duties further defined

A second census of the Levites is taken for a different purpose. In chapter 3 all the male Levites one month and older were taken for the purpose of setting them aside as substitutes for the firstborn males of the rest of Israel. In chapter 4 the male Levites between thirty and fifty years old are to be counted in order to assign them duties regarding the tent of meeting, its contents, and furnishings. The responsibilities of the three clans, which were briefly mentioned in 3:25-26, 31, 36-37, are now specified in greater detail.

The Kohathites, who have the most honorable responsibility, are discussed first. They are to carry the sacred objects that are housed in the tent of meeting along with their utensils (4:4, 15). No Levite may touch these sacred objects, however, not even the Kohathites. Thus the priests, Aaron and his sons, must first prepare these objects for transport (4:5-14). These priests take down the curtain that screens the ark of the covenant from view and use it to cover the ark. Then they are to wrap the ark in two additional coverings and insert the poles by which the Kohathites may carry the ark without touching it.

⁴This is the task of the Kohathites in the tent of meeting: the most sacred objects. ⁵In breaking camp, Aaron and his sons shall go in and take down the screening curtain and cover the ark of the covenant with it. ⁶Over these they shall put a cover of yellow-orange skin, and on top of this spread an all-violet cloth and put the poles in place. ⁷On the table of the Presence they shall spread a violet cloth and put on it the plates and cups, as well as the bowls and pitchers for libations; the established bread offering shall remain on the table. ⁸Over these they shall spread a scarlet cloth and cover it with a covering of yellow-orange skin, and put the poles in place. ⁹They shall use a violet cloth to cover the menorah of the light with its lamps, tongs, and trays, as well as the various containers of oil from which it is supplied. ¹⁰The menorah with all its utensils they shall then put in a covering of yellow-orange skin, and place on a litter. ¹¹Over the golden altar they shall spread a violet cloth, and cover this also with a covering of yellow-orange skin, and put the poles in place. ¹²Taking the utensils of the sanctuary service, they shall put them all in violet cloth and cover them with a covering of yellow-orange skin. They shall then place them on a litter. ¹³After cleansing the altar of its ashes, they shall spread a purple cloth over it. ¹⁴On this they shall put all the utensils with which it is served: the fire pans, forks, shovels, basins, and all the utensils of the altar. They shall then spread a covering of yellow-orange skin over this, and put the poles in place.

¹⁵Only after Aaron and his sons have finished covering the sacred objects and all their utensils on breaking camp, can the Kohathites enter to carry them. But they shall not touch the sacred objects;

The first covering is a yellow-orange skin (*tahash*), probably either dolphin skins or leather; the second covering is an "all-violet," or perfectly violet cloth. Violet or purple cloth is valuable because the dye is difficult to obtain. Thus the ark is covered richly. The table of the Presence on which the bread offering is laid along with the bread and the other utensils is to be covered in similar fashion, with violet and crimson cloths and the yellow-orange skin. The table too is provided with poles for carrying.

The menorah, along with its lamps, tongs for holding the wicks, oil containers, and trays for pouring the oil are wrapped in two coverings and placed on a litter. The incense altar is doubly covered and its carrying poles inserted; the other utensils are also doubly wrapped and placed on a litter. Finally, the bronze altar of sacrifice is cleansed of the ashes from burnt offerings and covered with a purple cloth. Then all its utensils—forks for turning and removing the meat of the sacrifice, basins for blood and other juices, fire pans and shovels for the coals—are covered with a yellow-orange skin and placed on top of the altar. The altar is also provided with poles for carrying.

if they do they will die. These, then, are the objects in the tent of meeting that the Kohathites shall carry.

¹⁶Eleazar, son of Aaron the priest, shall be in charge of the oil for the light, the fragrant incense, the established grain offering, and the anointing oil. He shall be in charge of the whole tabernacle with all the sacred objects and utensils that are in it.

¹⁷The LORD said to Moses and Aaron: ¹⁸Do not let the group of Kohathite clans perish from among the Levites. ¹⁹That they may live and not die when they approach the most sacred objects, this is what you shall do for them: Aaron and his sons shall go in and assign to each of them his task and what he must carry; ²⁰but the Kohathites shall not go in to look upon the sacred objects even for an instant, or they will die.

²¹The LORD said to Moses: ²²Take a census of the Gershonites also, by ancestral houses and clans, ²³enrolling all between thirty and fifty years of age who will join the personnel to do the work in the tent of meeting. ²⁴This is the task of the clans of the Gershonites, what they must do and what they must carry: ²⁵they shall carry the curtains of the tabernacle, the tent of meeting with its covering and the outer wrapping of yellow-orange skin, the curtain at the entrance of the tent of meeting, ²⁶the hangings of the court, the curtain at the entrance to the gate of the court that encloses both the tabernacle and the altar, together with their ropes and all other objects necessary for their use. Whatever is to be done to maintain these things, they shall do. ²⁷The service of the Gershonites shall be entirely under the direction of Aaron and his sons, with regard to what they must carry and what they must do; you shall list for them by name what they are to carry. ²⁸This, then,

All of this careful wrapping and covering is done by the priests to protect the Kohathites, because any non-priest, even a Kohathite, who touches these sacred objects will die (4:15, 18-19). No one but the priests may even look upon these holy things, even for an instant (4:20). The Hebrew word used to describe this "instant" means "a swallowing" (*balaᶜ*); the English equivalent would be the blink of an eye. So the sacred objects are prepared by the priests for the Kohathites to carry. The objects that are too sacred even for the Kohathites to carry—the oils, incense, and grain offering—are to be carried by the priest Eleazar, who is in charge of everything regarding the transport of the altar.

The tasks of the Gershonites (4:22-28) and the Merarites (4:29-33) are described more simply because the objects they carry are not so sacred and thus not so dangerous. The Gershonites carry all the fabric of the tent of meeting, the hangings and draperies. The Merarites carry the boards and braces, all the solid objects that form the structure of the tent of meeting. These two clans are under the supervision of the priest Ithamar.

is the task of the clans of the Gershonites in the tent of meeting; and they shall be under the supervision of Ithamar, son of Aaron the priest.

²⁹The Merarites, too, you shall enroll by clans and ancestral houses, ³⁰enrolling all between thirty and fifty years of age who will join the personnel to maintain the tent of meeting. ³¹This is what they shall be responsible for carrying, with respect to all their service in the tent of meeting: the boards of the tabernacle with its bars, columns and pedestals, ³²and the columns of the surrounding court with their pedestals, pegs and ropes, including all their accessories and everything for their maintenance. You shall list by name the objects they shall be responsible for carrying. ³³This, then, is the task of the clans of the Merarites with respect to all their service in the tent of meeting under the supervision of Ithamar, son of Aaron the priest.

Number of Adult Levites. ³⁴So Moses and Aaron and the leaders of the community enrolled the Kohathites, by clans and ancestral houses, ³⁵all between thirty and fifty years of age who will join the personnel to work in the tent of meeting; ³⁶their enrollment by clans was two thousand seven hundred and fifty. ³⁷Such was the enrollment of the clans of the Kohathites, everyone who was to serve in the tent of meeting, whom Moses enrolled, together with Aaron, as the LORD directed through Moses.

³⁸As for the enrollment of the Gershonites, by clans and ancestral houses, ³⁹all between thirty and fifty years of age who will join the personnel to work in the tent of meeting—⁴⁰their enrollment by clans and ancestral houses was two thousand six hundred and thirty. ⁴¹Such was the enrollment of the clans of the Gershonites, everyone who was to serve in the tent of meeting, whom Moses enrolled, together with Aaron, as the LORD directed.

⁴²As for the enrollment of the clans of the Merarites, by clans and ancestral houses, ⁴³all from thirty up to fifty years of age who will join the personnel to work in the tent of meeting—⁴⁴their enrollment by clans was three thousand two hundred. ⁴⁵Such was the enrollment

4:34-49 Number of adult Levites

The males between thirty and fifty years old belonging to these three clans must be counted in order to enroll them for this service regarding the tent of meeting (see 4:2-3). The Kohathites number 2,750, the Gershonites 2,630, and the Merarites 3,200. The total number of Levites available for service at the tent of meeting is 8,580. The minimum age for service noted here is thirty (see also 1 Chr 23:3). In chapter 8 the minimum age for Levitical service is given as twenty-five (Num 8:24), and in Chronicles it is twenty (1 Chr 23:24, 27; 2 Chr 31:17; cf. Ezra 3:8). This discrepancy may reflect different sources or different practices at different times. It also suggests that there may have been a lengthy period of training before a young Levite was allowed to perform the duties regarding the tent of meeting.

of the clans of the Merarites, whom Moses enrolled, together with Aaron, as the LORD directed through Moses.

⁴⁶As for the total enrollment of the Levites, which Moses and Aaron and the Israelite leaders had made, by clans and ancestral houses, ⁴⁷all between thirty and fifty years of age who were to undertake tasks of service or transport for the tent of meeting—⁴⁸their total enrollment was eight thousand five hundred and eighty. ⁴⁹As the LORD directed through Moses, they gave each of them their assign-

ments for service and for transport; just as the LORD had commanded Moses.

5 **The Unclean Expelled.** ¹The LORD said to Moses: ²Order the Israelites to expel from camp everyone with a scaly infection, and everyone suffering from a discharge, and everyone who has become unclean by contact with a corpse. ³Male and female alike, you shall expel them. You shall expel them from the camp so that they do not defile their camp, where I dwell in their midst. ⁴This the Israelites did, expelling them from

---

The narrator is careful to note that this count was made at the Lord's direction through Moses (4:37, 41, 45). Everything they did was in obedience to the Lord's command to Moses (4:49). Censuses taken without the Lord's command do not turn out well (cf. Exod 30:12; 2 Sam 24).

5:1-4 The unclean expelled

The holy God, symbolized by the tent of meeting, is present in the midst of the Israelite encampment. Thus the people must be holy and whatever threatens that holiness must be expelled or healed. The chapter begins with the "unwholeness" of disease and death. God's holiness is the source of life; disease and death must be removed from the camp.

Three groups are to be expelled: those with a scaly skin infection, those suffering from abnormal genital discharges, and those who have touched a corpse. The detailed legislation regarding scaly skin infections is outlined in Leviticus 13–14. This condition is not to be equated with Hansen's disease, commonly called leprosy. Rather it is any condition that renders the skin scaly and hard. According to this legislation in Numbers the person so affected must be expelled from the camp, not because of fear of infection but because the scaly skin is a sign of death. These persons are allowed to return to the camp only after the priest has declared them clean and the proper sacrifices have been offered (see Lev 13–14).

Men or women afflicted with abnormal genital discharges, pus or bleeding, form the second group. (This legislation does not apply to normal menstruation or seminal emission.) The abnormal genital discharge is a sign of contradiction: at the place where life is engendered, there is an indication of disease and death. According to Leviticus, these persons are allowed to

the camp; just as the LORD had commanded Moses, so the Israelites did.

Unjust Possession. ⁵The LORD said to Moses: ⁶Tell the Israelites: If a man or a woman commits any offense against another person, thus breaking faith with the LORD, and thereby becomes guilty, ⁷that person shall confess the wrong that has been done, make restitution in full, and in addition give one fifth of its value to the one that has been wronged. ⁸However, if there is no next of kin, one to whom restitution can be made, the restitution shall be made to the LORD and shall fall to the priest; this is apart from the ram of atonement with which the priest makes atonement for the guilty individual. ⁹Likewise, every contribution

---

return to the camp seven days after the affliction ceases; they too must offer a designated sacrifice (see Lev 15:1-15, 25-30).

The third group has become unclean by contact with a corpse, the ultimate sign of death. (See Num 19:11-22 for the full legislation.) This group includes those who perform the needed care of washing, dressing, and burying the body. These persons may re-enter the camp after they have performed the necessary purification rites on the third and seventh days after contact with a corpse (see Num 19:11-22).

5:5-10 Unjust possession

If external afflictions render a person impure, broken relationships do so even more. The next situation is clearly universal. The offender may be a *man or woman* (5:6). This inclusive phrase is unusual in biblical law (see Exod 21:28-29; Lev 13:29, 38; 20:27; Num 6:2; Deut 17:2, 5); usually "man" is the only one named. Also, the one offended is identified as any *ʾadam*, any human being.

The wrong has to do with misappropriation of property, cheating, or stealing. The offender must confess the wrong, offer a sacrifice of atonement, and make restitution with twenty percent interest (5:7-8). But a problem arises if the one wronged is dead. In that case the restitution must be paid to the next of kin, the redeemer (Hebrew *goʾel*). This redeemer is responsible to ransom a person who has been sold into slavery or to buy back the ancestral land that had been lost through debt (Lev 25:25-26, 48-49). The redeemer is also called to avenge a person's death (Num 35:18-21, 26-28; Deut 19:5-6, 11-13). Possible redeemers include father, mother, daughter, son, brother, uncle, or first cousin.

What happens if the wronged person is not only dead but has no redeemer? Then the restitution belongs to God (5:8). The priest accepts it in God's name. Whatever priest accepts the offering has the right to keep the offering (5:9-10).

among the sacred offerings that the Israelites present to the priest will belong to him. [10]Each shall possess his own sacred offerings; what is given to a priest shall be his.

Ordeal for Suspected Adultery. [11]The LORD said to Moses: [12]Speak to the Israelites and tell them: If a man's wife goes astray and becomes unfaithful to him [13]by virtue of a man having intercourse with her in secret from her husband and she is able to conceal the fact that she has defiled herself for lack of a witness who might have caught her in the act; [14]or if a man is overcome by a feeling of jealousy that makes him suspect his wife, and she has defiled herself; or if a man is overcome by a feeling of jealousy that makes him suspect his wife and she has not defiled herself—[15]then the man shall bring his wife to the priest

as well as an offering on her behalf, a tenth of an ephah of barley meal. However, he shall not pour oil on it nor put frankincense over it, since it is a grain offering of jealousy, a grain offering of remembrance which recalls wrongdoing.

[16]The priest shall first have the woman come forward and stand before the LORD. [17]In an earthen vessel he shall take holy water, as well as some dust from the floor of the tabernacle and put it in the water. [18]Making the woman stand before the LORD, the priest shall uncover her head and place in her hands the grain offering of remembrance, that is, the grain offering of jealousy, while he himself shall hold the water of bitterness that brings a curse. [19]Then the priest shall adjure the woman, saying to her, "If no other man has had intercourse

5:11-31 Ordeal for suspected adultery

If the broken relationship is marriage, the situation is even more critical and must be healed if the encampment of God's people is to remain holy. The husband has the right to take action and divorce his wife if he has evidence of adultery or serious sexual misconduct (see Deut 24:1). If, however, he only suspects his wife but does not have evidence, he may subject her to an ordeal. If she fails the test, she is dishonored and physically impaired and he may divorce her. If she passes the test, she is exonerated and he may not divorce her.

The ritual for the ordeal combines several elements: an oath, a magical water test, and a grain offering. The grain offering is necessary because one may never appear before God empty-handed (Exod 23:15; Deut 16:16). This offering differs from the ordinary grain offering in that it is made of barley meal instead of coarse flour (semolina), no oil is smeared on it, and no frankincense accompanies it. The offering is starker because it is an "offering of jealousy" and a memorial of wrongdoing. It is offered for the woman (5:15) after she has taken the oath and before she drinks the bitter water (5:25-26).

with you, and you have not gone astray by defiling yourself while under the authority of your husband, be immune to this water of bitterness that brings a curse. ²⁰But if you have gone astray while under the authority of your husband, and if you have defiled yourself and a man other than your husband has had intercourse with you"—²¹so shall the priest adjure the woman with this imprecation—"may the Lord make you a curse and malediction among your people by causing your uterus to fall and your belly to swell! ²²May this water, then, that brings a curse, enter your bowels to make your belly swell and your uterus fall!" And the woman shall say, "Amen, amen!" ²³The priest shall put these curses in writing and shall then wash them off into the water of bitterness, ²⁴and he will have the woman drink the water of bitterness that brings a curse, so that the water that brings a curse may enter into her to her bitter hurt. ²⁵But first the priest shall take the grain offering of jealousy from the woman's hand, and having elevated the grain offering before the Lord, shall bring it to the altar, ²⁶where he shall take a handful of the grain offering as a token offering and burn it on the altar. Only then shall he have the woman drink the water. ²⁷Once he has had her drink the water, if she has defiled herself and been unfaithful to her husband, the water that brings a curse will enter into her to her bitter hurt, and her belly will swell and her uterus will fall, so that she will become a curse among her people. ²⁸If, however, the woman has not defiled

---

The oath is administered after the woman has been made to stand before the altar with her head uncovered and the grain offering in her hands. The action shames the woman, whose hair is uncovered and probably disheveled by a man not her husband. The husband is also shamed by this public display. The oath has two parts. The first is an oath of innocence. If she has not been unfaithful, the bitter water will not hurt her. The second part is a self-curse if she is guilty. The priest concludes with a curse that assumes the woman's guilt (5:21-22) and she swears her agreement to the two-part oath, "Amen, amen!"

The base for the water of bitterness is "holy water" (5:17; the only appearance of this phrase in the Old Testament). It may be water from the basin that is set between the tent of meeting and the altar (Exod 30:18; 40:30). Dust from the floor of the tabernacle is put into this water and the ink of the oath's words written by the priest is washed into it. The water thus symbolizes purification (the water from the basin) as well as death (dust). The dust and ink, no doubt, make the water taste bitter and suggest danger or poison. When the woman drinks the water, she is taking into herself the oath with its curse (ink) as well as physical elements from the sacred place (water and dust).

herself, but is still pure, she will be immune and will still be fertile.

²⁹This, then, is the ritual for jealousy when a woman goes astray while under the authority of her husband and defiles herself, ³⁰or when such a feeling of jealousy comes over a man that he becomes suspicious of his wife; he shall have her stand before the Lᴏʀᴅ, and the priest shall perform this entire ritual for her. ³¹The man shall be free from punishment, but the woman shall bear her punishment.

6 **Laws Concerning Nazirites.** ¹The Lᴏʀᴅ said to Moses: ²Speak to the Israelites and tell them: When men or women solemnly take the nazirite vow to dedicate themselves to the Lᴏʀᴅ, ³they shall abstain from wine and strong drink; they may neither drink wine vinegar, other vinegar, or any kind of grape juice, nor eat either fresh or dried grapes. ⁴As long as they are nazirites they shall not eat anything of the produce of the grapevine; not even the seeds or the skins. ⁵While they are under the nazirite

The effect of the water depends on the woman's guilt or innocence. If she is guilty, her uterus will fall and her belly swell. If she is innocent, the water will have no effect and, literally, "she will be sown with seed" (5:28). There are two possible meanings here. If the woman is pregnant and that is the reason that her husband suspected her, she will either miscarry if guilty or bear a healthy child if innocent. If the woman is not pregnant, she will either suffer a prolapsed uterus if guilty or remain fertile if innocent. In any case, the husband remains free of guilt even if he suspected his wife falsely.

The Code of Hammurabi (eighteenth century B.C.) also has a water ordeal for suspected adultery. "If the 'finger is pointed' at a man's wife about another man, but she is not caught sleeping with the other man, she shall jump into the river for her husband" (no. 132, translated by L.W. King; see also nos. 131, 133, 143). If she drowns, she was guilty; if she survives, she is innocent.

6:1-21 Laws concerning Nazirites

Another relationship is so important that its disruption also causes defilement of the sanctuary: the relationship between the Nazirite and God. Nazirites willingly take a vow to dedicate their lives to God for a certain time (6:1-8). (The stories of Samson [Judg 13:4-5] and Samuel [1 Sam 1:11, 22] indicate that a Nazirite vow could also be taken for life, but the legislation in this chapter is primarily directed to those who make the vow only for a time.) It is specifically stated that either men or women are permitted to make this vow. (The phrase "men or women" is rare in biblical law, appearing only here in 6:2 and in Exod 21:28-29; Lev 13:29, 38; 20:27; Num 5:6; Deut 17:2, 5; 29:17.)

vow, no razor shall touch their hair. Until the period of their dedication to the Lord is over, they shall be holy, letting the hair of their heads grow freely. ⁶As long as they are dedicated to the Lord, they shall not come near a dead person. ⁷Not even for their father or mother, sister or brother, should they defile themselves, when these die, since their heads bear their dedication to God. ⁸As long as they are nazirites they are holy to the Lord.

⁹If someone dies very suddenly in their presence, defiling their dedicated heads, they shall shave their heads on the day of their purification, that is, on the seventh day. ¹⁰On the eighth day they shall bring two turtledoves or two pigeons to the priest at the entrance of the tent of meeting. ¹¹The priest shall offer up the one as a purification offering and the other as a burnt offering, thus making atonement for them for the sin they committed with respect to the corpse. On the same day they shall reconsecrate their heads ¹²and rededicate themselves to the Lord for the period of their dedication, bringing a yearling lamb as a reparation offering. The previous period is not valid, because they defiled their dedicated heads.

¹³This is the ritual for the nazirites: When the period of their dedication is complete they shall go to the entrance of the tent of meeting, ¹⁴bringing their offerings to the Lord, one unblemished

---

The language in this section is particularly dense, with significant words repeated several times. The root *nzr*, from which "nazirite" is derived, means "to separate or set apart"; it occurs twenty-four times in 6:1-21. Related roots, which have similar meanings, are interwoven with *nzr*. The root *ndr*, usually translated "vow" or "dedicate," occurs six times; the common root *qdsh*, usually translated "holy" but which connotes setting apart, occurs four times. This rich interweaving of words describing the dedication of the Nazirite to God indicates the solemnity of this action.

Three restrictions characterize the Nazirite: abstention from wine and any other grape product including raisins, refraining from cutting the hair, and avoidance of any dead body including that of any immediate family member. Drinking wine, especially to the point of intoxication, was associated with the Canaanites, particularly their agricultural way of life. Critiques of the agricultural economy appear in the story of Noah's drunkenness (Gen 9:20-27) and in the seventh-century protest of the Rechabites, who insisted on maintaining their nomadic way of life, neither building houses nor planting crops nor drinking wine (see Jer 35).

Hair was considered an extension of a person's vitality. Not cutting the hair was a way of preserving strength (see Samson, especially Judg 16:17-20). Offering one's hair to God symbolized the total dedication of one's life.

yearling lamb for a burnt offering, one unblemished yearling ewe lamb for a purification offering, one unblemished ram as a communion offering, [15]and a basket of unleavened cakes of bran flour mixed with oil and of unleavened wafers spread with oil, along with their grain offerings and libations. [16]The priest shall present them before the LORD, and shall offer up the purification offering and the burnt offering for them. [17]He shall then offer up the ram as a communion sacrifice to the LORD, along with the basket of unleavened cakes, and the priest will offer the grain offering and libation. [18]Then at the entrance of the tent of meeting the nazirite shall shave his or her dedicated head, take the hair of the dedicated head, and put it in the fire under the communion sacrifice. [19]After the nazirite has shaved off the dedicated hair, the priest shall take a boiled shoulder of the ram, as well as one unleavened cake from the basket and one unleavened wafer, and shall put them in the hands of the nazirite. [20]The priest shall then elevate them as an elevated offering before the LORD. They are an

---

The strict legislation concerning avoidance of a corpse is a protection against a cult of the dead like that practiced in the rest of the ancient Near East. The dead were not transformed into immortal gods and were not to be worshiped. In this society where there was no belief in resurrection, the dead were not considered even to remain as part of the human community. Holiness has to do with life, not death, and the consecrated Nazirite must thus avoid any contact with the dead.

The Nazirite who transgressed these three prohibitions, even accidentally, had to go through a seven-day ritual of purification and begin the whole period of Nazirite consecration again (6:9-12). The hair must be shaved off because the consecration has been lost. No doubt this shaved hair is to be burned with the sacrifice just as it is at the normal end of the period of consecration (6:18). Sacrifices must be offered to God: first an offering to purify the sanctuary, which has been defiled, and then a burnt offering to restore the relationship with God. Finally a lamb is offered as reparation for the broken vow. Only then can the person begin again to be a Nazirite for whatever period of time had been initially set.

A complicated ritual signifies the end of the designated period of time for the Nazirite vow. One does not lightly move from a consecrated state to ordinary life. In addition to the purification offering and the burnt offering, the person brings a ram for a communion offering along with grain and drink offerings. These last offerings symbolize an ongoing sharing of life with God, the gift of *shalom*, peace and well-being. After these are offered, the consecrated hair is shaved off and burned in the fire of the sacrifice. Only then may the former Nazirite return to an ordinary way of life.

offering belonging to the priest, along with the brisket of the elevated offering and the leg of the contribution. Only after this may the nazirite drink wine.

²¹This, then, is the law for the nazirites, that is, what they vow as their offering to the LORD in accord with their dedication, apart from anything else which their means may allow. In keeping with the vow they take so shall they do, according to the law of their dedication.

The Priestly Blessing. ²²The LORD said to Moses: ²³Speak to Aaron and his sons and tell them: This is how you shall bless the Israelites. Say to them:

²⁴The LORD bless you and keep you!
²⁵The LORD let his face shine upon
      you, and be gracious to you!
²⁶The LORD look upon you kindly
      and give you peace!

²⁷So shall they invoke my name upon the Israelites, and I will bless them.

The detailed instructions for Nazirites and the solemnity of the ritual at the end of the period of dedication indicate the degree of holiness attached to this vow. The restriction regarding contact with the dead, for example, is more stringent even than that placed on the priests (Lev 21:1-4); it is as strict as the demands on the high priest (Lev 21:11). Nazirites were a living symbol of holiness in the midst of God's holy people.

6:22-27 The priestly blessing

The blessing assigned to the priests, descendants of Aaron, is very old and is still in common use. Similar blessings have been found on a jar from the eighth century B.C. at Kuntillet ʿAjrud in the upper Sinai Peninsula and on small silver pieces, possibly amulets, in seventh-century graves in the Hinnom Valley outside Jerusalem. The second-century sage, Ben Sira, describes the high priest's daily blessing: "Then coming down he would raise his hands / over all the congregation of Israel; / The blessing of the LORD would be upon his lips, / the name of the LORD would be his glory. / The people would again fall down / to receive the blessing of the Most High" (Sir 50:20-21). The blessing found here in Numbers is currently used at the end of Evening Praise in the Liturgy of the Hours and sometimes as the concluding blessing of the Eucharist. In the Roman Lectionary it is the first reading for New Year's Day.

God's blessing signifies a sharing in God's life and power. To be blessed by God is not only to be endowed with spiritual grace; it is also to receive material abundance. In Genesis human beings are blessed with fertility and the gift of land (see Gen 1:28; 27:27-29; 35:9-12). God's blessing also brings prosperity and peace. To be blessed by God is to be strengthened to live as true human beings, images of God.

33

7 **Offerings of the Tribal Leaders.** ¹Now, when Moses had completed the erection of the tabernacle, he anointed and consecrated it with all its equipment, as well as the altar with all its equipment. After he anointed and consecrated them, ²an offering was made by the tribal leaders of Israel, who were heads of ancestral houses, the same leaders of the tribes who supervised those enrolled. ³The offering they brought before the LORD consisted of six wagons for baggage and twelve oxen, that is, a wagon for every two tribal leaders, and an ox for each. These they presented before the tabernacle.

⁴The LORD then said to Moses: ⁵Accept their offering, that these things may be put to use to maintain the tent of meeting. Assign them to the Levites, to each according to his duties. ⁶So Moses accepted the wagons and oxen, and assigned them to the Levites. ⁷He gave two wagons and four oxen to the Gershonites according to their duties, ⁸and four wagons and eight oxen to the Merarites according to their duties, under the supervision of Ithamar, son of Aaron the priest. ⁹He gave none to the Kohathites, because they were responsible for maintenance of the sacred objects that had to be carried on their shoulders.

¹⁰For the dedication of the altar also, the tribal leaders brought offerings when it was anointed; the leaders presented their offering before the altar. ¹¹But the LORD said to Moses: Let one leader each day present his offering for the dedication of the altar.

¹²The one who presented his offering on the first day was Nahshon, son of Amminadab, of the tribe of Judah. ¹³His offering consisted of one silver plate weighing a hundred and thirty shekels and one silver basin weighing seventy shekels according to the sanctuary shekel, both filled with bran flour mixed with oil for a grain offering; ¹⁴one gold cup of ten shekels' weight filled with incense; ¹⁵one bull from the herd, one ram, and one yearling lamb for a burnt offering; ¹⁶one goat for a purification offering; ¹⁷and two bulls, five rams, five he-goats, and five yearling lambs for a communion sacrifice. This was the offering of Nahshon, son of Amminadab.

¹⁸On the second day Nethanel, son of Zuar, tribal leader of Issachar, made his offering. ¹⁹He presented as his offering one silver plate weighing a hundred and thirty shekels and one silver basin weighing seventy shekels according to the sanctuary shekel, both filled with bran flour mixed with oil for a grain offering; ²⁰one gold cup of ten shekels' weight filled with incense; ²¹one bull from the herd, one ram, and one yearling

---

7:1-88 Offerings of the tribal leaders

This chapter is a flashback to the day of dedication of the tabernacle: the first day of the first month of the second year from the departure from Egypt, according to Exodus 40:2-17. Thus this chapter describes events a month earlier than the first chapter of Numbers (see 1:1). All the legal traditions in Leviticus and Numbers 1–5 are, in a sense, outside of time. Here we resume the temporal sequence.

lamb for a burnt offering; [22]one goat for a purification offering; [23]and two bulls, five rams, five he-goats, and five yearling lambs for a communion sacrifice. This was the offering of Nethanel, son of Zuar.

[24]On the third day it was the turn of the tribal leader of the Zebulunites, Eliab, son of Helon. [25]His offering consisted of one silver plate weighing a hundred and thirty shekels and one silver basin weighing seventy shekels according to the sanctuary shekel, both filled with bran flour mixed with oil for a grain offering; [26]one gold cup of ten shekels' weight filled with incense; [27]one bull from the herd, one ram, and one yearling lamb for a burnt offering; [28]one goat for a purification offering; [29]and two bulls, five rams, five he-goats, and five yearling lambs for a communion sacrifice. This was the offering of Eliab, son of Helon.

[30]On the fourth day it was the turn of the tribal leader of the Reubenites, Elizur, son of Shedeur. [31]His offering consisted of one silver plate weighing a hundred and thirty shekels and one silver basin weighing seventy shekels according to the sanctuary shekel, both filled with bran flour mixed with oil for a grain offering; [32]one gold cup of ten shekels' weight filled with incense; [33]one bull from the herd, one ram, and one yearling lamb for a burnt offering; [34]one goat for a purification offering; [35]and two bulls, five rams, five he-goats, and five yearling lambs for a communion sacrifice. This was the offering of Elizur, son of Shedeur.

[36]On the fifth day it was the turn of the tribal leader of the Simeonites, Shelumiel, son of Zurishaddai. [37]His offering consisted of one silver plate weighing a hundred and thirty shekels and one silver basin weighing seventy shekels according to the sanctuary shekel, both filled with bran flour mixed with oil for a grain offering; [38]one gold cup of ten shekels' weight filled with incense; [39]one bull from the herd, one ram, and one yearling lamb for a burnt offering; [40]one goat for a purification offering; [41]and two bulls, five rams, five he-goats, and five yearling lambs for a communion sacrifice. This was the offering of Shelumiel, son of Zurishaddai.

The tabernacle and all its equipment, including the altar, have been anointed. Anointing with sacred oil was a common practice in the ancient Near East to set something apart for special use or to indicate the special status of a person such as a king or priest. This dedication (Hebrew *hanukkah*) prepares the sacred space for its intended use as a meeting place between God and the covenant people.

The first set of offerings brought by the tribal leaders (see commentary on 1:4-19) consists of the means of transportation for the tabernacle and all its equipment. The wagons and oxen are assigned to the ancestral houses of the Levites according to their responsibilities (see commentary on 3:14-40; 4:1-33). The Kohathites do not need wagons and oxen since they carry on their shoulders the sacred objects from inside the tabernacle.

⁴²On the sixth day it was the turn of the tribal leader of the Gadites, Eliasaph, son of Reuel. ⁴³His offering consisted of one silver plate weighing a hundred and thirty shekels and one silver basin weighing seventy shekels according to the sanctuary shekel, both filled with bran flour mixed with oil for a grain offering; ⁴⁴one gold cup of ten shekels' weight filled with incense; ⁴⁵one bull from the herd, one ram, and one yearling lamb for a burnt offering; ⁴⁶one goat for a purification offering; ⁴⁷and two bulls, five rams, five he-goats, and five yearling lambs for a communion sacrifice. This was the offering of Eliasaph, son of Reuel.

⁴⁸On the seventh day it was the turn of the tribal leader of the Ephraimites, Elishama, son of Ammihud. ⁴⁹His offering consisted of one silver plate weighing a hundred and thirty shekels and one silver basin weighing seventy shekels according to the sanctuary shekel, both filled with bran flour mixed with oil for a grain offering; ⁵⁰one gold cup of ten shekels' weight filled with incense; ⁵¹one bull from the herd, one ram, and one yearling lamb for a burnt offering; ⁵²one goat for a purification offering; ⁵³and two bulls, five rams, five he-goats, and five yearling lambs for a communion sacrifice. This was the offering of Elishama, son of Ammihud.

⁵⁴On the eighth day it was the turn of the tribal leader of the Manassites, Gamaliel, son of Pedahzur. ⁵⁵His offering consisted of one silver plate weighing a hundred and thirty shekels and one silver basin weighing seventy shekels according to the sanctuary shekel, both filled with bran flour mixed with oil for a grain offering; ⁵⁶one gold cup of ten shekels' weight filled with incense; ⁵⁷one bull from the herd, one ram, and one yearling lamb for a burnt offering; ⁵⁸one goat for a purification offering; ⁵⁹and two bulls, five rams, five he-goats, and five yearling lambs for a communion sacrifice. This was the offering of Gamaliel, son of Pedahzur.

⁶⁰On the ninth day it was the turn of the tribal leader of the Benjaminites, Abidan, son of Gideoni. ⁶¹His offering consisted of one silver plate weighing a hundred and thirty shekels and one silver basin weighing seventy shekels according to the sanctuary shekel, both

The next section (7:10-88) seems to be the verbal presentation of a table of offerings. Each of the twelve tribal leaders is named and his offerings listed (see Figure 3, p. 14, for the order of tribes). From the third tribal leader on, there are no verbs. The use of numbers is out of the ordinary: instead of "two bulls, five rams, five he-goats," for example, the Hebrew says: "bulls–two, rams–five, he-goats–five." The donations are listed, not according to the ordinary order of sacrifice with items for the purification offering first, but according to value with the gold and silver items first and then the animals large and small. It is easiest to imagine someone reading this list aloud from a table. At the end (7:84-88), the "bottom line" is read, the total of all the offerings.

filled with bran flour mixed with oil for a grain offering; [62]one gold cup of ten shekels' weight filled with incense; [63]one bull from the herd, one ram, and one yearling lamb for a burnt offering; [64]one goat for a purification offering; [65]and two bulls, five rams, five he-goats, and five yearling lambs for a communion sacrifice. This was the offering of Abidan, son of Gideoni.

[66]On the tenth day it was the turn of the tribal leader of the Danites, Ahiezer, son of Ammishaddai. [67]His offering consisted of one silver plate weighing a hundred and thirty shekels and one silver basin weighing seventy shekels according to the sanctuary shekel, both filled with bran flour mixed with oil for a grain offering; [68]one gold cup of ten shekels' weight filled with incense; [69]one bull from the herd, one ram, and one yearling lamb for a burnt offering; [70]one goat for a purification offering; [71]and two bulls, five rams, five he-goats, and five yearling lambs for a communion sacrifice. This was the offering of Ahiezer, son of Ammishaddai.

[72]On the eleventh day it was the turn of the tribal leader of the Asherites, Pagiel, son of Ochran. [73]His offering consisted of one silver plate weighing one hundred and thirty shekels and one silver basin weighing seventy shekels ac-

cording to the sanctuary shekel, both filled with bran flour mixed with oil for a grain offering; [74]one gold cup of ten shekels' weight filled with incense; [75]one bull from the herd, one ram, and one yearling lamb for a burnt offering; [76]one goat for a purification offering; [77]and two bulls, five rams, five he-goats, and five yearling lambs for a communion sacrifice. This was the offering of Pagiel, son of Ochran.

[78]On the twelfth day it was the turn of the tribal leader of the Naphtalites, Ahira, son of Enan. [79]His offering consisted of one silver plate weighing a hundred and thirty shekels and one silver basin weighing seventy shekels according to the sanctuary shekel, both filled with bran flour mixed with oil for a grain offering; [80]one gold cup of ten shekels' weight filled with incense; [81]one bull from the herd, one ram, and one yearling lamb for a burnt offering; [82]one goat for a purification offering; [83]and two bulls, five rams, five he-goats, and five yearling lambs for a communion sacrifice. This was the offering of Ahira, son of Enan.

[84]These were the offerings for the dedication of the altar, given by the tribal leaders of Israel on the occasion of its anointing: twelve silver plates, twelve silver basins, and twelve gold cups.

Each tribe brings the same offering, regardless of the size of the tribe. Each tribe shares equally in the worship of God at the tabernacle. The tribes appear, not in birth order as in chapter 1, but in the same sequence as chapter 2 with Judah appearing first (see Figure 3, p. 14, and commentary on ch. 2). It seems that these sacrifices are not being made at the dedication; rather their offerings provide the resources for future offerings of all the major sacrifices in the priestly tradition (see Lev 6–7) except the guilt offering.

⁸⁵Each silver plate weighed a hundred and thirty shekels, and each silver basin seventy, so that all the silver of these vessels amounted to two thousand four hundred shekels, according to the sanctuary shekel. ⁸⁶The twelve gold cups that were filled with incense weighed ten shekels apiece, according to the sanctuary shekel, so that all the gold of the cups amounted to one hundred and twenty shekels. ⁸⁷The animals for the burnt offerings were, in all, twelve bulls, twelve rams, and twelve yearling lambs, with their grain offerings; those for the purification offerings were twelve goats. ⁸⁸The animals for the communion sacrifices were, in all, twenty-four bulls, sixty rams, sixty he-goats, and sixty yearling lambs. These, then, were the offerings for the dedication of the altar after it was anointed.

The Voice. ⁸⁹When Moses entered the tent of meeting to speak with God, he heard the voice addressing him from above the cover on the ark of the covenant, from between the two cherubim; and so it spoke to him.

8 The Menorah. ¹The LORD said to Moses: ²Speak to Aaron and say: "When you set up the menorah-lamps, have the seven lamps throw their light in front of the menorah." ³Aaron did so, setting up the menorah-lamps to face the area in front of the menorah, just as the LORD had commanded Moses. ⁴This is the construction of the menorah:

7:89 The voice

The final verse of this chapter is a transition from the twelve days of offerings outside the tabernacle to the arrangement of the inside. The sacred place is identified as the tent of meeting. In contrast to the Priestly description earlier (e.g., 2:17; 3:38) where the tent is in the center of the camp, here the tent is outside the camp (also at 11:24-27; 12:4-5; see introduction: tent of meeting/tabernacle). God comes to the tent to speak with Moses (see Exod 33:7-11). God is revealed only by word, only by voice. The voice comes from between the cherubim, guardians of the ark. God's instructions continue in the next chapter with the phrase so frequent in Numbers 1–10: "The LORD said to Moses."

8:1-4 The menorah

The final detail in preparing the tabernacle is the instruction on the function of the menorah, the seven-branched lampstand. The making of the menorah was described in Exodus (25:31-40; 37:17-24). Regarding its use, the Israelites are all commanded to supply the oil (Lev 24:2), but only the priest Aaron (and his sons) may care for this sacred object (Exod 30:7-8). It must be so situated that the light shines toward the altar, the sign of God's presence. This is how God instructs Aaron (8:1-2), and this is what Aaron does (8:3).

hammered gold, from its base to its bowls it was hammered; according to the pattern which the Lord had shown Moses, so he made the menorah.

Purification of the Levites. ⁵The Lord said to Moses: ⁶Take the Levites from among the Israelites and cleanse them. ⁷This is what you shall do to them to cleanse them. Sprinkle them with the water of purification, have them shave their whole bodies and wash their garments, and so cleanse themselves. ⁸Then they shall take a bull from the herd, along with its grain offering of bran flour mixed with oil; and you shall take another bull from the herd for a purification offering. ⁹Bringing the Levites before the tent of meeting, you shall assemble also the whole community of the Israelites. ¹⁰When you have brought the Levites before the Lord, the Israelites shall lay their hands upon them. ¹¹Aaron shall then present the Levites before the Lord as an elevated offering from the Israelites, that they may perform the service of the Lord. ¹²The Levites in turn shall lay their hands on the heads of the bulls, offering one as a purification offering and the other as a burnt offering to the Lord, to make atonement for the Levites. ¹³Then you shall have the Levites stand before Aaron and his sons, and you shall present them as an elevated offering to the Lord; ¹⁴thus you shall separate the Levites from the rest of the Israelites, and the Levites shall belong to me.

8:5-22 Purification of the Levites

The Levites must now be prepared for their ministry. The ritual begins with three outward signs of purification. They are sprinkled with water, shave their whole bodies, and wash their clothes (see Exod 19:10). Then a sacrifice of purification is offered. The congregation, through designated representatives, lays hands on the Levites, designating them as special ministers and offering them to God. The Levites in turn lay hands on the two bulls, one for the purification sacrifice and the other for the burnt offering. Thus the Levites are identified with the animals for sacrifice. Aaron the priest offers the Levites to God in the name of the people and sacrifices the two bulls according to the appropriate sacrifices. The first is a sacrifice to purify the Levites; the second is a whole burnt offering, asking God to accept their service.

The Levites are cleansed but not "consecrated" or "ordained" as are the Aaronide priests (see introduction, Levites, p. 9). They are not sprinkled nor touched with sacrificial blood or anointed with oil. They do not have the power or status of the priests. They may neither touch the sacred objects nor offer sacrifice or enter the tabernacle. This designation of the Levites' duties reflects the period from Josiah onward (seventh century B.C.) after all sacrificial worship was limited to the temple (see also Ezek 44).

¹⁵Only then shall the Levites enter upon their service in the tent of meeting, when you have cleansed them and presented them as an elevated offering. ¹⁶For they, among the Israelites, are totally dedicated to me; I have taken them for myself in place of everyone that opens the womb, the firstborn of all the Israelites. ¹⁷Indeed, all the firstborn among the Israelites, human being and beast alike, belong to me; I consecrated them to myself on the day I killed all the firstborn in the land of Egypt. ¹⁸But I have taken the Levites in place of all the firstborn Israelites; ¹⁹and from among the Israelites I have given to Aaron and his sons these Levites, who are to be dedicated, to perform the service of the Israelites in the tent of meeting and to make atonement for them, so that no plague may strike among the Israelites should they come too near the sanctuary.

²⁰This, then, is what Moses and Aaron and the whole community of the Israelites did with respect to the Levites; the Israelites did exactly as the LORD had commanded Moses concerning them. ²¹When the Levites had purified themselves and washed their garments, Aaron presented them as an elevated offering before the LORD, and made atonement for them to cleanse them. ²²Only then did they enter upon their service in the tent of meeting under the supervision of Aaron and his sons. Exactly as the LORD had commanded Moses concerning the Levites, so it was done with regard to them.

Age Limits for Levitical Service. ²³The LORD said to Moses: ²⁴This is the rule for the Levites. Everyone twenty-five years old or more shall join the personnel in the service of the tent of meeting. ²⁵But everyone fifty on up shall retire from the work force and serve no more. ²⁶They shall assist their fellow Levites in the tent of meeting in performing their duties, but they shall not do the work. This, then, is how you are to regulate the duties of the Levites.

The Levites are set aside, however, as God's own possession. They substitute for the firstborn of all the Israelites (see commentary on 3:5-13). They, who have been purified by sacrifice, form a bridge between the Israelites and the holiness of God and serve as a protection for the Israelites who may not come too near the tabernacle. They also serve as assistants to the priests.

This is what God commands (8:5-19); this is what is done (8:20-22).

8:23-26 Age limits for Levitical service

Levites are to begin their service at age twenty-five and retire to minor duties at age fifty. This instruction differs from the age limits in the census (4:2-3), where the Levites undertake their tasks at age thirty. Perhaps there was a period of training before full responsibility was given to a young Levite.

9 **Second Passover.** ¹The LORD said to Moses in the wilderness of Sinai, in the first month of the second year following their departure from the land of Egypt: ²Tell the Israelites to celebrate the Passover at the prescribed time. ³In the evening twilight of the fourteenth day of this month you shall celebrate it at its prescribed time, in accord with all its statutes and regulations. ⁴So Moses told the Israelites to celebrate the Passover, ⁵and they did celebrate the Passover on the fourteenth day of the first month during the evening twilight in the wilderness of Sinai. Just as the LORD had commanded Moses, so the Israelites did.

⁶There were some, however, who were unclean because of a human corpse and so could not celebrate the Passover that day. These men came up to Moses and Aaron that same day ⁷and they said to them, "Although we are unclean because of a human corpse, why should we be deprived of presenting the LORD's offering at its prescribed time along with other Israelites?" ⁸Moses answered them, "Wait so that I can learn what the LORD will command in your regard."

⁹The LORD then said to Moses: ¹⁰Speak to the Israelites: "If any one of you or of your descendants is unclean because of a human corpse, or is absent on a journey, you may still celebrate the LORD's

---

9:1-14 Second Passover

This chapter concludes the flashback that began in 7:1. This section is set on the day that the tabernacle was finished, the first day of the *first* month of the second year after the people left Egypt (cf. Exod 40:17), whereas Numbers begins in the *second* month of the second year after the departure from Egypt.

Passover, the memorial of the deliverance from Egypt, is the most significant liturgical celebration for God's covenant people. Passover celebrations are described only a few times in the Old Testament, but all of these are at critical junctures in the people's history. The first Passover is an anticipatory celebration of deliverance (Exod 12; cf. Num 33:3). The second Passover is described here as the people prepare to leave Sinai and continue their trek through the wilderness. The third mention of a Passover celebration occurs just after Joshua and the people cross the Jordan River to enter the Promised Land (Josh 5).

There are only three other stories describing the observance of this important liturgy: Hezekiah's attempt during his reform to reunite with the remaining people of the northern kingdom after the Assyrian invasion (2 Chr 30), at the conclusion of Josiah's reform (2 Kgs 23//2 Chr 35), and after the Babylonian exile when the second temple was finished (Ezra 6:19-22). Instructions for how to observe the festival are found in Exodus 34, Leviticus 23, Numbers 28, and Deuteronomy 16 (cf. Ezek 45).

Passover. ¹¹But you shall celebrate it in the second month, on the fourteenth day of that month during the evening twilight, eating it with unleavened bread and bitter herbs, ¹²and not leaving any of it over till morning, nor breaking any of its bones, but observing all the statutes of the Passover. ¹³However, anyone who is clean and not away on a journey, who yet fails to celebrate the Passover, shall be cut off from the people, for not presenting the LORD's offering at the prescribed time. That person shall bear the consequences of this sin.

¹⁴"If an alien who lives among you would celebrate the LORD's Passover, it shall be celebrated according to the statutes and regulations for the Passover. You shall have the same law for the resident alien as for the native of the land."

The familiar pattern of the Lord's command (9:2-4) and the people's obedience (9:5) appears again. The regulations, which are outlined in detail in Exodus 12, are stated here only briefly. A problem arises, however: what to do with those who are ritually unclean? Moses waits for a command from the Lord.

The Lord's instruction extends not only to those who cannot celebrate because of ritual uncleanness, but to everyone who finds it impossible to keep the Passover feast for whatever reason. This is the only feast that all Israel is required to keep. No one is to be excused from this memorial of Israel's creation as a people. Anyone who is prevented from celebrating at the appropriate time during the first month of the year must keep the feast at the prescribed time during the second month. Anyone who neglects to keep this feast is to be cut off from the people. To be "cut off" is equivalent to death. By failing to keep the Passover the offender has symbolically already separated from the community's life and identity.

The reasons listed that persons may be unable to keep the Passover at the appropriate time are: ritual uncleanness, travel, or non-Israelite status. Those who are ritually unclean are put outside the camp for a prescribed number of days and are not allowed to participate in any worship (see 5:2-3). The other two reasons, however, suggest that these laws belong to a time after Israel is well settled in the land. Travel is a difficulty only if the celebration of Passover is limited to a certain place. In the time of Josiah (seventh century) all formal worship was centralized in the Jerusalem temple. As for the third reason, resident aliens were part of Israel only after they had their own land. During the wilderness period they themselves were "resident aliens." Throughout the Pentateuch we find similar evidence that later laws were inserted into earlier material. Almost the whole legal tradition in particular gravitated toward the story of Israel's stay at Sinai (Exod 19–Num 10).

The Fiery Cloud. [15]On the day when the tabernacle was erected, the cloud covered the tabernacle, the tent of the covenant; but from evening until morning it took on the appearance of fire over the tabernacle. [16]It was always so: during the day the cloud covered the tabernacle and at night had the appearance of fire. [17]Whenever the cloud rose from the tent, the Israelites would break camp; wherever the cloud settled, the Israelites would pitch camp. [18]At the direction of the LORD the Israelites broke camp, and at the LORD's direction they pitched camp. As long as the cloud stayed over the tabernacle, they remained in camp.

[19]Even when the cloud lingered many days over the tabernacle, the Israelites kept the charge of the LORD and would not move on. [20]Yet if it happened the cloud was over the tabernacle only for a few days, at the direction of the LORD they stayed in camp; and at the LORD's direction they broke camp. [21]If it happened the cloud remained there only from evening until morning, when the cloud rose in the morning, they would break camp. Whether the cloud lifted during the day or the night they would then break camp. [22]Whether the cloud lingered over the tabernacle for two days or for a month or longer, the

9:15-23 The fiery cloud

In the middle of the chapter is another reminder that this is the first day of the *first* month of the second year after the departure from Egypt, the day on which the tabernacle was completed. The time at Sinai is coming to an end. The previous description of Passover bound together the section from Exodus 12 to Numbers 9; now the story of God's taking possession of the tabernacle, symbolized by the cloud, is repeated (see Exod 40:34-38).

The cloud is a common biblical symbol for God's presence. The radiant cloud both reveals and conceals God's presence. When the Israelites were encamped by the sea, God protected them by day in a pillar of cloud and by night in a pillar of fire (Exod 13:21-22; 14:19-20, 24; cf. Deut 1:33; Ps 78:14). Apparently the fire burns constantly in the middle of the cloud but is invisible in daylight. The glory of the Lord appeared as a shining cloud when Aaron announced that God would give the people bread (manna; Exod 16:10). When Moses received the Ten Commandments, the cloud covered Mount Sinai (Exod 24:15-18). When Moses went to the tent of meeting to speak with God, the cloud signaled God's arrival (Exod 33:9-10). When the priests dedicated the temple that Solomon had built in the tenth century, the cloud filled the temple so completely that the priests could not continue their ministry (1 Kgs 8:10-11). The cloud as a symbol for God's glorious presence is also common in the rest of the ancient Near East as well as in Christian iconography. The halo around a holy person's head is a stylized image of the cloud.

Israelites remained in camp and did not break camp; but when it lifted, they broke camp. ²³At the direction of the LORD they pitched camp, and at the LORD's direction they broke camp; they kept the charge of the LORD, as the LORD directed them through Moses.

10 **The Silver Trumpets.** ¹The LORD said to Moses: ²Make two trumpets of silver, making them of hammered silver, for you to use in summoning the community and in breaking camp. ³When both are blown, the whole community shall gather round you at the entrance of the tent of meeting; ⁴but when one of them is blown, only the tribal leaders, the heads of the clans of Israel, shall gather round you. ⁵When you sound the signal, those encamped on the east side shall break camp; ⁶when you sound a second signal, those encamped on the south side shall break camp; when you sound a

---

God, present in the cloud, is the leader of the people on their journey from Sinai to the Promised Land. When the cloud moves, the people follow; when the cloud stops, the people rest. They go nowhere except where the cloud leads. They are completely obedient to the Lord's direction.

10:1-10 The silver trumpets

The final preparation for Israel's departure from Sinai is the making of the two silver trumpets. Josephus, a first-century Jewish historian, describes these silver trumpets as somewhat less than eighteen inches long (less than a cubit), straight, and bell-shaped at the end (*Antiq.* III, xii, 6). Their sound must have been piercing. These straight trumpets (Hebrew *hatsotserah*) are different from the ram's horn (*shofar*) and the *yobel* (also a ram's horn, from which "jubilee" gets its name). Trumpets are used to announce feasts and heighten the celebration (Ps 98:6; Ezra 3:10; Neh 12:35, 41; and throughout Chr) as well as to summon warriors to battle (Num 31:6; Hos 5:8).

The Aaronide priests are assigned to blow the trumpets. Different signals are sounded on them. The difference between the signal for an assembly (10:3-4, 7), the signal for breaking camp and departing (10:5-6), and the signal for battle (10:9) is not described. Possibly the signal for an assembly is only a long sound and signals for the other two events are a series of tones in a certain rhythm.

The trumpets are not only signals for the people, however. When the trumpet is sounded for war, God remembers the people and saves them (10:9). The trumpet sound during liturgical celebrations serves as a memorial for the people before God (10:10). Throughout the Old Testament God's remembering means well-being for the people. When God remembers Noah, the floodwaters begin to abate (Gen 8:1). When God remembers the covenant, he calls Moses to deliver the people from Egyptian oppression

45

third signal, those encamped on the west side shall break camp; when you sound a fourth signal, those encamped on the north side shall break camp. Thus shall the signal be sounded for them to break camp. ⁷But in calling forth an assembly you are to blow a blast, without sounding the signal.

⁸The sons of Aaron, the priests, shall blow the trumpets; this is prescribed forever for you and your descendants. ⁹When in your own land you go to war against an enemy that is attacking you, you shall sound the alarm on the trumpets, and you shall be remembered before the LORD, your God, and be saved from your foes. ¹⁰And when you rejoice on your festivals, and your new-moon feasts, you shall blow the trumpets over your burnt offerings and your communion sacrifices, so that this serves as a reminder of you before your God. I, the LORD, am your God.

II. Departure, Rebellion, and Wandering in the Wilderness for Forty Years

Departure from Sinai. ¹¹In the second year, on the twentieth day of the second month, the cloud rose from the tabernacle of the covenant, ¹²and the Israelites moved on from the wilderness of Sinai by stages, until the cloud came to rest in the wilderness of Paran.

¹³The first time that they broke camp at the direction of the LORD through Moses, ¹⁴the divisional camp of the Judahites, arranged in companies, was the first to set out. Over its whole company was Nahshon, son of Amminadab, ¹⁵with Nethanel, son of Zuar, over the company of the tribe of Issacharites, ¹⁶and Eliab,

---

(Exod 2:24). When God remembers Hannah, she conceives Samuel (1 Sam 1:19-20). The trumpets become a signal for God to continue remembering just as the bow in the clouds does (Gen 9:16).

DEPARTURE, REBELLION, AND WANDERING IN THE WILDERNESS FOR FORTY YEARS

Numbers 10:11–25:18

10:11-28 Departure from Sinai

The Israelites, having arrived at Sinai on the first day of the third month after their departure from Egypt (Exod 19:1), now set out to continue their journey through the wilderness. They have been camped at Sinai almost a year. There they have made covenant with the Lord, broken the covenant by forging a golden calf (Exod 32:1-4), and been granted a new covenant (Exod 34:1-28). They have received the gift of the law, beginning with the Ten Commandments (Exod 20:1-17). Since all Israelite law is covenant law, the later law codes have also been inserted into the Sinai story; these laws form the bulk of material from Exodus 21, through Leviticus, to Numbers 10.

son of Helon, over the company of the tribe of Zebulunites. [17]Then, after the tabernacle was dismantled, the Gershonites and Merarites who carried the tabernacle set out. [18]The divisional camp of the Reubenites, arranged in companies, was the next to set out. Over its whole company was Elizur, son of Shedeur, [19]with Shelumiel, son of Zurishaddai, over the company of the tribe of Simeonites, [20]and Eliasaph, son of Reuel, over the company of the tribe of Gadites. [21]The Kohathites, who carried the sacred objects, then set out. Before their arrival the tabernacle would be erected. [22]The divisional camp of the Ephraimites set out next, arranged in companies. Over its whole company was Elishama, son of Ammihud, [23]with Gamaliel, son of Pedahzur, over the company of the tribe of Manassites, [24]and Abidan, son of Gideoni, over the company of the tribe of Benjaminites. [25]Finally, as rear guard for all the camps, the divisional camp of the Danites set out, arranged in companies. Over its whole company was Ahiezer, son of Ammishaddai, [26]with Pagiel, son of Ochran, over the company of the tribe of Asherites, [27]and Ahira, son of Enan, over the company of the tribe of Naphtalites. [28]This was the order of march for the Israelites, company by company, when they set out.

Now instructions for the rest of the journey have been given and the cloud has risen from the tabernacle of the covenant (so called because the ark is traditionally believed to have contained the tablets of the commandments; see Exod 25:16, 21; 40:20; Deut 10:2, 5; 1 Kgs 8:9; 2 Chr 6:11). It is time to move on.

The tribes set out in the order given in Numbers 2 (see Figure 3, p. 14). The Levitical clans join the march according to their respective duties. The Gershonites and Merarites, who carry the structural elements of the tabernacle (Num 4:21-33), set out after the first division led by the Judahites. They are to have the structure set up before the arrival of the Kohathites, who are carrying the sacred objects (Num 4:4-15) and who set out after the second division led by the Reubenites.

The journey will take the people from the wilderness of Sinai to the wilderness of Paran (10:12; 12:16). On the way they will camp at Taberah (11:3), Kibroth-hattaavah (perhaps the same place, 11:34); and Hazeroth (11:35). The exact location of these places is difficult to determine. It is generally accepted that Mount Sinai is Jebel Musa in the southern tip of the Sinai Peninsula. The wilderness of Paran is a more or less large area in the north-central part of the peninsula. Kadesh-barnea, in the wilderness of Zin, seems to be at the northern edge of the wilderness of Paran (20:1; cf. 13:26). See map on page 154.

Hobab as Guide. [29]Moses said to Hobab, son of Reuel the Midianite, Moses' father-in-law, "We are setting out for the place concerning which the LORD has said, 'I will give it to you.' Come with us, and we will be generous toward you, for the LORD has promised prosperity to Israel." [30]But he answered, "No, I will not come. I am going instead to the land of my birth." [31]Moses said, "Please, do not leave us; you know where we can camp in the wilderness, and you can serve as our guide. [32]If you come with us, we will share with you the prosperity the LORD will bestow on us."

Into the Wilderness. [33]From the mountain of the LORD they made a journey of three days, and the ark of the

---

10:29-32 Hobab as guide

The section from 1:1–10:28 represents priestly interests and is considered to be from the Priestly tradition. A pre-Priestly source, which seems actually to be a combination of several different traditions, begins with 10:29. Thus there are several contradictions evident in this section: Moses' father-in-law, who is named Jethro throughout most of Exodus (3:1; 4:18; 18:1-12) but Reuel in Exodus 2:18, is here called Hobab, who is the son of Reuel (cf. Judg 4:11). Moses asks him to be their guide, although God, signified by the cloud (9:15-23; 10:11-12) or the ark (10:33-34), is supposed to show them the way. The cloud itself forms a pillar (Exod 13:21-22; Num 12:5) or covers the tabernacle and/or the tent (Exod 40:34-38; Num 9:15-16), but appears rarely with the ark as it does here (Lev 16:2; cf. 16:13).

Perhaps this last item is not a contradiction, since the ark is to be set within the tabernacle (Exod 40:5, 21) and the cloud hovers over the people when the ark leads them (Num 10:34). But where is the ark found in the order of march? According to the detailed instructions from the Priestly tradition the ark is to be carried by the Kohathites (Num 4:4-5, 15) and they march behind the Reubenite division, close to the center of the line. In 10:33-36, however, the ark goes before the people.

These contradictions must be noted but need not be disturbing. They reveal the great respect of the ancient biblical editors for the traditions they have inherited. These editors seem to have operated according to the principle, "Don't throw anything away because it may contain some truth." When Christians gathered the books of the New Testament they had the same respect for sources. The four gospels contradict each other in many details, but the church has kept them all.

10:33-36 Into the wilderness

The ark of the covenant has many functions. It is a sign of God's abiding presence with the people. It is a throne for God (1 Sam 4:4; 2 Sam 6:2; 2

covenant of the LORD went before them for the three-day journey to seek out a resting place for them. ³⁴And the cloud of the LORD was over them by day when they set out from camp.

³⁵Whenever the ark set out, Moses would say,

"Arise, O LORD, may your enemies be scattered,
and may those who hate you flee before you."

³⁶And when it came to rest, he would say,

"Bring back, O LORD, the myriads of Israel's troops!"

11 **Discontent of the People.** ¹Now the people complained bitterly in the hearing of the LORD; and when he heard it his wrath flared up, so that the LORD's fire burned among them and consumed the outskirts of the camp. ²But when the people cried out to Moses, he prayed to the LORD and the fire died out. ³Hence that place was called Taberah, because there the fire of the LORD burned among them.

Kgs 19:15/Isa 37:16; Pss 80:2; 99:1; 1 Chr 13:6); God's footstool (1 Chr 28:2; Pss 99:5; 132:7); the Lord rides upon the cherubim (Pss 18:11; Ezek 10:18-20; 11:22). It is used as a palladium to be carried into battle (see 1 Sam 4–7). It is a container, holding the tablets of the commandments (Deut 10:2-5; 1 Kgs 8:9). In Christian tradition it is also thought to contain a jar of manna and Aaron's rod that blossomed (Heb 9:4). In Numbers 10 it is a symbol of God's guidance of the people through the wilderness.

The song of the ark is a battle song. The Lord advances into battle, scattering the enemies, and returns to camp with the army. The placement of the song here indicates that the journey from Sinai to the Promised Land will not be entirely peaceful.

11:1-15 Discontent of the people

The murmuring of the people that characterized the journey from Egypt to Mount Sinai returns and intensifies. In the period before their arrival at the covenant mountain they grumbled about genuine needs. They cried out and God, in response to Moses' prayer, gave them what they needed (see Exod 16–17). Now they complain where there is no need and their grumbling rouses God's anger. They have made covenant with the Lord and have experienced generous care for more than two years, but still they do not trust God to continue sustaining them. This is a critical moment in Israel's history. Will their lack of trust destroy the covenant? Moses, caught in the middle between a rebellious people and an angry God, must continually intercede for them.

The first murmuring story is told in general terms and functions as a pattern for the rest. The people complain, apparently for no good reason. God

⁴The riffraff among them were so greedy for meat that even the Israelites lamented again, "If only we had meat for food! ⁵We remember the fish we used to eat without cost in Egypt, and the cucumbers, the melons, the leeks, the onions, and the garlic. ⁶But now we are famished; we have nothing to look forward to but this manna."

⁷Manna was like coriander seed and had the appearance of bdellium. ⁸When they had gone about and gathered it up, the people would grind it between millstones or pound it in a mortar, then cook it in a pot and make it into loaves, with a rich creamy taste. ⁹At night, when the dew fell upon the camp, the manna also fell.

¹⁰When Moses heard the people, family after family, crying at the entrance of their tents, so that the LORD became very angry, he was grieved. ¹¹"Why do you treat your servant so badly?" Moses asked the LORD. "Why are you so displeased

overhears their grumbling and with blazing anger burns the outer edges of the encampment. After the people cry out, Moses prays and God quenches the fire. The event gives the place its name: The Burning (Taberah).

Thus the pattern is set: (1) the people complain for no good reason; (2) God punishes them in anger; (3) they cry out; (4) Moses prays for them and God removes the punishment; (5) finally they name the place for the event.

The second murmuring story in this chapter is more complex. Two issues are interwoven: the people's weariness with the manna and Moses' weariness with leadership. Food has been a cause for grumbling since they left Egypt (see Exod 16); now leadership becomes a primary source of conflict. The story begins with the food issue. The grumbling begins with the mixed crowd that left Egypt with the Israelites (see Exod 12:38).

The people complain that they are tired of manna; God's gift is not sufficient for their taste. According to Psalm 78 they cry out, "Can God spread a table in the desert?" (Ps 78:19). They remember fondly the meals in Egypt. Ironically they list the foods they got *without cost*, but forget that they paid with their slave labor. The second issue arises immediately. Moses hears their grumbling and voices his own complaint to God: "Why are you so displeased with me that you burden me with all this people?" Moses points out that he is not their mother; God is! God conceived them and gave them birth, so why does Moses have to nurse them? The people may be tired of manna, but Moses is tired of the people. He begs God to just let him die.

Imaging God as mother rather than father may seem surprising. Masculine images for God do outnumber feminine images in the Bible. This passage, however, is not the only biblical example of imaging God as mother (e.g., Ps 131; Isa 49:15; 66:13; Sir 4:10).

with me that you burden me with all this people? ¹²Was it I who conceived all this people? or was it I who gave them birth, that you tell me to carry them at my breast, like a nurse carrying an infant, to the land you have promised under oath to their fathers? ¹³Where can I get meat to give to all this people? For they are crying to me, 'Give us meat for our food.' ¹⁴I cannot carry all this people by myself, for they are too heavy for me. ¹⁵If this is the way you will deal with me, then please do me the favor of killing me at once, so that I need no longer face my distress."

The Seventy Elders. ¹⁶Then the LORD said to Moses: Assemble for me seventy of the elders of Israel, whom you know to be elders and authorities among the people, and bring them to the tent of meeting. When they are in place beside you, ¹⁷I will come down and speak with you there. I will also take some of the spirit that is on you and will confer it on them, that they may share the burden of the people with you. You will then not have to bear it by yourself.

¹⁸To the people, however, you shall say: "Sanctify yourselves for tomorrow, when you shall have meat to eat. For in the hearing of the LORD you have cried, 'If only we had meat for food! Oh, how well off we were in Egypt!' Therefore the LORD will give you meat to eat, ¹⁹and you will eat it, not for one day, or two

11:16-23 The seventy elders

The Lord outlines a plan to resolve both issues. Moses is to gather seventy elders at the tent of meeting where God will bestow on them a share of the spirit that is on Moses (see Exod 24:1-11). Second, Moses is to prepare the people for the gift of meat.

Seventy is a common biblical number for completion or for inclusion of the Gentiles (see Gen 10). Here it seems to be an indication that Moses will have plenty of help. In Exodus 18, Moses' father-in-law advised him to appoint minor judges to help him in settling disputes. In this passage God promises to give a share of Moses' charismatic gift to reputable elders so that they may share his leadership tasks. Apparently Moses' grumbling came out of a real need as did the people's grumbling before they arrived at Sinai. Thus God will supply what he needs.

The tone of God's reply regarding the people's desire for variety in their diet signals that the response to this complaint will not end so happily. God sounds like a disgusted mother: "You want meat? You will get meat! You will eat it until it comes out your noses!" Why is God so angry? The people want to undo the exodus, God's gracious rescue of them. They want to undo the covenant: they would rather be people of Egypt than people of God. Moses attempts to intercede by reasoning with God: "Do you know how many people we have? Can you really give them that much meat?" God replies, "Wait and see!"

days, or five, or ten, or twenty days, ²⁰but for a whole month—until it comes out of your very nostrils and becomes loathsome to you. For you have rejected the LORD who is in your midst, and in his presence you have cried, 'Why did we ever leave Egypt?'"

²¹But Moses said, "The people around me include six hundred thousand soldiers; yet you say, 'I will give them meat to eat for a whole month.' ²²Can enough sheep and cattle be slaughtered for them? If all the fish of the sea were caught for them, would they have enough?" ²³The LORD answered Moses: Is this beyond the LORD's reach? You shall see now whether or not what I have said to you takes place.

The Spirit on the Elders. ²⁴So Moses ▶ went out and told the people what the LORD had said. Gathering seventy elders of the people, he had them stand around the tent. ²⁵The LORD then came down in the cloud and spoke to him. Taking some of the spirit that was on Moses, he bestowed it on the seventy elders; and as the spirit came to rest on them, they prophesied but did not continue.

²⁶Now two men, one named Eldad and the other Medad, had remained in the camp, yet the spirit came to rest on them also. They too had been on the list, but had not gone out to the tent; and so they prophesied in the camp. ²⁷So, when a young man ran and reported to Moses, "Eldad and Medad are prophesying in

---

The number of people Moses claims to lead agrees with the number given when Israel set out from Egypt: 600,000 men, not counting women, children, and the "crowd of mixed ancestry" that went with them (Exod 12:37-38). The number is no doubt inflated. If the others were included, the count would reach approximately two million, an impossible number for this trek across the desert.

11:24-30 The spirit on the elders

Now the final resolution of the two issues begins. The leadership question is treated first. Moses gathers the seventy elders at the tent of meeting where the Lord appears in the cloud (see Exod 33:9-10). The location of the tent outside the camp and the appearance of the Lord in the cloud indicate the source of the passage to be the pre-Priestly tradition. (In the Priestly tradition the tent is in the center of the camp; see Num 2:2). Moses has been filled with the spirit of prophecy throughout his ministry. The description of his call in Exodus 3 is a model for the call of later prophets (see Isa 6; Jer 1; Ezek 1–3). Now the Lord will take some of that spirit and bestow it on the elders who are to be his assistants. The effect is immediate: they fall into a prophetic trance. Saul will have a similar experience when the spirit of God comes upon him (1 Sam 10:10-13; 19:20-23). This ecstatic experience is not lasting, but their commission as assistants to Moses continues.

the camp," [28]Joshua, son of Nun, who from his youth had been Moses' aide, said, "My lord, Moses, stop them." [29]But Moses answered him, "Are you jealous for my sake? If only all the people of the LORD were prophets! If only the LORD would bestow his spirit on them!" [30]Then Moses retired to the camp, along with the elders of Israel.

The Quail. [31]There arose a wind from the LORD that drove in quail from the sea and left them all around the camp site, to a distance of a day's journey and at a depth of two cubits upon the ground. [32]So all that day, all night, and all the next day the people set about to gather in the quail. Even the one who got the least gathered ten homers of them. Then they spread them out all around the camp. [33]But while the meat was still between their teeth, before it could be chewed, the LORD's wrath flared up against the people, and the LORD struck them with a very great plague. [34]So that place was named Kibroth-hattaavah, because it was there that the greedy people were buried.

[35]From Kibroth-hattaavah the people set out for Hazeroth, where they stayed.

The spirit of God, however, cannot be constricted by human limitations. Two of the elders were on the list but for some reason did not go out to the tent of meeting. The spirit found them anyway and they too fell into a prophetic state. Joshua wanted Moses to stop them. But Moses has no desire to control God's spirit, nor is he protective of his own prophetic gift. He wishes that all God's people might be prophets. In the next chapter God will reconfirm Moses' own special status.

11:31-35 The quail

The leadership question has been settled; now it remains to satisfy the appetite of the people. So God again sent a wind. A wind sent by God had also split the Red Sea and turned it into dry land so that the people could cross (Exod 14:21-22). A mighty wind hovered over the waters when God began to create (Gen 1:2). This time the wind sent by God drives in an abundance of quail. Underlying this story is the fact that many birds migrate across the Sinai Peninsula. Often they are exhausted from the trip across the Mediterranean. So many quail are driven in by the wind that they pile up on the ground a yard deep! (A cubit is about eighteen inches.) An alternate view is that they can fly only about a yard above the ground. In either case, the weakened birds surround the camp for the distance of a day's journey.

For two days the greedy people gather as many quail as they can. Everyone got at least forty to fifty bushels of them. God, however, is still angry. Before they have even swallowed their feast, they are struck with a great plague. They wanted the tasty foods of Egypt; instead they suffer a plague just as Egypt did. The place, according to the pattern, is named

12 Jealousy of Aaron and Miriam.

¹Miriam and Aaron spoke against Moses on the pretext of the Cushite woman he had married; for he had in fact married a Cushite woman. ²They complained, "Is it through Moses alone that the LORD has spoken? Has he not spoken through us also?" And the LORD heard this. ³Now the man Moses was very humble, more than anyone else on earth. ⁴So at once the LORD said to Moses and Aaron and Miriam: Come out, you three, to the tent of meeting. And the three of them went. ⁵Then the LORD came down in a column of cloud, and standing at the entrance of the tent, called, "Aaron and Miriam." When both came forward, ⁶the LORD said: Now listen to my words:

If there are prophets among you,
    in visions I reveal myself to
        them,
    in dreams I speak to them;
⁷Not so with my servant Moses!
Throughout my house he is worthy
        of trust:
    ⁸face to face I speak to him,
        plainly and not in riddles.
The likeness of the LORD he be-
        holds.

---

for the event: The Graves of Greed, Kibroth-hattaavah. The survivors then continue their journey, stopping at Hazeroth. (See Ps 78:26-31 for another version of this story.)

12:1-9 Jealousy of Aaron and Miriam

In chapter 11, Moses expressed a wish that all God's people might be prophets. Now the two other desert leaders, Miriam and Aaron, challenge Moses' singular authority as a prophet: "Is it through Moses alone that the LORD has spoken?" (12:2). A prophet is first and foremost God's messenger, one who speaks in God's name. Moses has certainly done that. But are there not others in the wilderness community who also speak God's word? Moses, truly humble, seems to pray for that (11:29).

The challenge is introduced with what seems to be an unrelated issue, Moses' marriage to a Cushite woman. Cush is somewhere south of Egypt and is usually identified with Ethiopia. This woman is almost certainly not Zipporah, who is identified as a Midianite. It is not likely that the problem is Moses' taking a second wife. Abraham had three wives (Sara, Hagar, and Keturah); Jacob had two wives and two concubines (Rachel, Leah, Bilhah, and Zilpah). David and Solomon will have multiple wives.

The problem is also not one of race, even though a Cushite may be black. Racial discrimination against blacks is not known in biblical times. The difficulty may center on the fact that the great lawgiver has married a foreign woman. Especially after the Babylonian exile there is a fear of marrying foreign women (see Ezra 9–10; Neh 13).

Why, then, do you not fear to speak against my servant Moses? ⁹And so the LORD's wrath flared against them, and he departed.

Miriam's Punishment. ¹⁰Now the cloud withdrew from the tent, and there was Miriam, stricken with a scaly infection, white as snow! When Aaron turned toward Miriam and saw her stricken with snow-white scales, ¹¹he said to Moses, "Ah, my lord! Please do not charge us with the sin that we have foolishly committed! ¹²Do not let her be like the stillborn baby that comes forth from its mother's womb with its flesh half consumed." ¹³Then Moses cried to the LORD, "Please, not this! Please, heal her!" ¹⁴But the LORD answered Moses: Suppose her father had spit in her face, would she not bear her shame for seven

---

The danger of foreign women also appears in reports of other events: Rebekah's fear that Jacob will marry a Hittite or Canaanite (Gen 27:46; 28:1), Moabite and Midianite women leading Israel astray (Num 25:1, 6-18), Solomon seduced into idolatry by foreign wives (1 Kgs 11:1-2). All these stories were probably written during or after the Babylonian exile. If the fact that the wife is foreign is the problem, however, why is Zipporah the Midianite not a problem also? Among the patriarchs, Judah married a Canaanite (Gen 38:2) and Joseph an Egyptian (Gen 41:45). The book of Ruth (perhaps also postexilic) identifies a Moabite woman as David's ancestor. The difficulty with Moses' Cushite wife remains a mystery.

The Lord responds to the other difficulty: prophetic status in the wilderness community. The three leaders are summoned to the tent of meeting where the Lord appears in the column of cloud (see Exod 33:9-10; Num 11:24-25). He addresses Aaron and Miriam directly and declares in no uncertain terms the priority of Moses. Other prophets receive the Lord's message in visions or dreams, but the Lord speaks to Moses face to face (literally "mouth to mouth"). Moses sees the form or the likeness of the Lord. By contrast, Israel at Sinai saw no form but only heard God's voice (Deut 4:12). The Lord declares that Moses is truly unique. Aaron and Miriam may have some prophetic gifts, and indeed each is named "prophet" (Exod 7:1; 15:20); however, they will never equal Moses.

12:10-16 Miriam's punishment

The complaint of Miriam and Aaron is another murmuring story in this series. They have complained where there was no need, and thus the anger of God is roused against them. Miriam is struck with a scaly infection and thus must be expelled from the camp (see Lev 13:1-46; Num 5:1-4). Aaron pleads with Moses who begs God to heal her (thus following the pattern set in Num 11:1-3). As is the case in the other murmuring stories in Numbers,

days? Let her be confined outside the camp for seven days; afterwards she may be brought back. ¹⁵So Miriam was confined outside the camp for seven days, and the people did not start out again until she was brought back.

¹⁶After that the people set out from Hazeroth and encamped in the wilderness of Paran.

13 **The Twelve Scouts.** ¹The LORD said to Moses: ²Send men to reconnoiter the land of Canaan, which I am giving the Israelites. You shall send

one man from each ancestral tribe, every one a leader among them. ³So Moses sent them from the wilderness of Paran, at the direction of the LORD. All of them were leaders among the Israelites. ⁴These were their names:

from the tribe of Reuben, Sham-
mua, son of Zaccur;
⁵from the tribe of Simeon, Shaphat,
son of Hori;
⁶from the tribe of Judah, Caleb, son
of Jephunneh;
⁷from the tribe of Issachar, Igal;

God heeds Moses' plea, but not before some of the punishment has been carried out. Miriam will suffer excommunication for seven days.

Why is Miriam punished and Aaron not? There is a hint that the story may originally have been only about Miriam and Moses. It is odd to find Miriam's name before Aaron's. More convincingly, however, the Hebrew verb in 12:1 is feminine singular even though the subject is the compound "Miriam and Aaron" saying literally, "Miriam and Aaron, she spoke against Moses." "Aaron" seems to have been added to the sentence. All the remaining verbs are plural and Aaron is mentioned first in verses 4 and 5.

Is there a deeper meaning here also? It surely is not that a woman cannot hope to be a prophet. Both Deborah (Judg 4:4) and Huldah (2 Kgs 22:14) will later be called prophets. Or is Miriam punished because she is also challenging Aaron's priestly authority? Aaron has been set aside as priest and the ancestor of the priestly clan (Exod 28–29; 40:12-15; Num 17:16–18:7). Is Aaron spared the uncleanness because of his priestly status? This text too remains a mystery.

13:1-24 The twelve scouts

The story of the twelve scouts as it appears here represents a combination of sources and viewpoints. An early version appears in verses 17b-20, 22-24, and 27-31. Another version, possibly Priestly, is represented in verses 1-17a, 25-26, 32-33. In the early tradition the people are at Kadesh (see 13:26) and the object of the expedition is to discover whether an invasion of Canaan from the south is possible. In the Priestly tradition the community is encamped in the wilderness of Paran (see 13:3, 26) and arrives in Kadesh only in 20:1. The scouts are to explore the whole land that God

⁸for the Josephites, from the tribe of Ephraim, Hoshea, son of Nun;

⁹from the tribe of Benjamin, Palti, son of Raphu;

¹⁰from the tribe of Zebulun, Gaddiel, son of Sodi;

¹¹for the Josephites, from the tribe of Manasseh, Gaddi, son of Susi;

¹²from the tribe of Dan, Ammiel, son of Gemalli;

¹³from the tribe of Asher, Sethur, son of Michael;

¹⁴from the tribe of Naphtali, Nahbi, son of Vophsi;

¹⁵from the tribe of Gad, Geuel, son of Machi.

¹⁶These are the names of the men whom Moses sent to reconnoiter the land. But Hoshea, son of Nun, Moses called Joshua.

¹⁷In sending them to reconnoiter the land of Canaan, Moses said to them, "Go up there in the Negeb, up into the highlands, ¹⁸and see what kind of land it is and whether the people living there are strong or weak, few or many. ¹⁹Is the country in which they live good or bad? Are the towns in which they dwell open or fortified? ²⁰Is the soil fertile or barren, wooded or clear? And do your best to get some of the fruit of the land." It was then the season for early grapes.

²¹So they went up and reconnoitered the land from the wilderness of Zin as far as where Rehob adjoins Lebo-hamath. ²²Going up by way of the Negeb, they reached Hebron, where Ahiman, Sheshai and Talmai, descendants of the Anakim, were. (Now Hebron had been built seven years before Zoan in Egypt.) ²³They also reached the Wadi Eshcol, where they cut down a branch with a single cluster of grapes on it, which two of them carried on a pole, as well as some pomegranates and figs. ²⁴It was because of the cluster

---

has promised. Both traditions are attempting to explain why the Israelites did not enter the Promised Land from the south shortly after the exodus and Sinai experiences.

The story begins with the Priestly tradition. God gives the order to spy out the land and Moses and the people obey. There is another list of tribal leaders similar in form to the list in Numbers 1:4-19, but the names are different. Hoshea, representative of the tribe of Ephraim, is renamed Joshua by Moses. The two names are similar: Hoshea means "he saves"; Joshua means "The Lord saves." Although Joshua appeared in chapter 11, it sounds here as if he is just being introduced.

A pre-Priestly tradition begins in the middle of verse 17. The scouts are instructed to determine the possible success of an attack: the fortifications of the towns and the strength of the inhabitants. They are also to evaluate the fertility of the land. From Kadesh they travel through the Negeb as far as Hebron, thus exploring only the southern part of the Promised Land. (The P tradition inserts v. 21, extending the scouts' journey to the northern limits

the Israelites cut there that they called the place Wadi Eshcol.

Their Report. ²⁵They returned from reconnoitering the land forty days later. ²⁶Proceeding directly to Moses and Aaron and the whole community of the Israelites in the wilderness of Paran at Kadesh, they made a report to them and to the whole community, showing them the fruit of the land. ²⁷They told Moses: "We came to the land to which you sent us. It does indeed flow with milk and honey, and here is its fruit. ²⁸However, the people who are living in the land are powerful, and the towns are fortified and very large. Besides, we saw descendants of the Anakim there. ²⁹Amalekites live in the region of the Negeb; Hittites, Jebusites and Amorites dwell in the highlands, and Canaanites along the sea and the banks of the Jordan."

³⁰Caleb, however, quieted the people before Moses and said, "We ought to go up and seize the land, for we can

of the land; see 34:8.) They discover that the land is indeed rich; to prove this they cut down a cluster of grapes so large it has to be carried on a pole by two men. They name the place "Grape Cluster" (Hebrew: *eshcol*).

13:25-33 Their return

In the early version of the scouts' return (13:27-31), they report the results of their search into the two questions of fertile land and possible conquest. First they show the immense cluster of grapes and declare that this is indeed a land of milk and honey (see Exod 3:8, 17; 13:5; 33:3). Then they acknowledge that the cities are indeed fortified and the inhabitants strong. Some are descendants of the legendary Anakim, widely believed to be giants. Others are the traditional enemies mentioned throughout the settlement period: Amalekites, Hittites, Jebusites, and Amorites (see Exod 17:8-16; 33:2; Josh 3:10). If the Israelites invade they will be surrounded by powerful foes! Apparently the people respond in fear, but Caleb, the Judahite scout, reassures them that, if they attack, they will prevail. The other scouts, however, counter his encouragement with a prediction of certain failure.

The Priestly tradition shifts the emphasis of the scouts' report (13:32-33). Instead of describing the goodness of the land, they announce that this land consumes its inhabitants (a direct contradiction of verse 27). This land is like Sheol that swallows up the unwary (see Prov 1:12; Isa 5:14). They heighten the terrifying appearance of the inhabitants: They are Nephilim ("fallen ones," translated "giants" in the Septuagint), descendants of gods and human women (see Gen 6:1-4); they are so huge that the scouts felt like grasshoppers. The scouts' discouraging report is called *dibba* in Hebrew. This word *dibba* usually connotes slander. God has promised this land and the scouts are disparaging it. Their report is a rejection of God's gift.

59

"Grapes from Canaan." Illustration by Charles Foster, 1897.

certainly prevail over it." ³¹But the men who had gone up with him said, "We cannot attack these people; they are too strong for us." ³²They spread discouraging reports among the Israelites about the land they had reconnoitered, saying, "The land that we went through and reconnoitered is a land that consumes its inhabitants. And all the people we saw there are huge. ³³There we saw the Nephilim (the Anakim are from the Nephilim); in our own eyes we seemed like mere grasshoppers, and so we must have seemed to them."

14 **Threats of Revolt.** ¹At this, the whole community broke out with loud cries, and the people wept into the night. ²All the Israelites grumbled against Moses and Aaron, the whole community saying to them, "If only we had died in the land of Egypt," or "If only we would die here in the wilderness! ³Why is the LORD bringing us into this land only to have us fall by the sword? Our wives and little ones will be taken as spoil. Would it not be better for us to return to Egypt?" ⁴So they said to one another, "Let us appoint a leader and go back to Egypt."

⁵But Moses and Aaron fell prostrate before the whole assembled community of the Israelites; ⁶while Joshua, son of Nun, and Caleb, son of Jephunneh, who had been among those that reconnoitered

14:1-9 Threats of revolt

The story continues with the Priestly editing of the earlier story (14:1-7a). The Israelite community wails in despair at the grim report of the scouts. Once more the murmuring begins. Now, however, the complaint is not about conditions in the wilderness, but about the difficulties of entering the Promised Land. In the earlier stories the people remembered how wonderful Egypt seemed; now they would prefer even to die in the wilderness. Moses prayed to die in chapter 11; now the people pray to die. Anything is better than attempting to take possession of the land that God has promised them. The only solution they can think of in their distress is to replace Moses as leader and return to Egypt. They not only want to forfeit God's gift of the land; they also want to undo God's liberation of them in the exodus event. They are undoing the covenant relationship with God from Abraham to Moses.

Moses and Aaron fall on their faces at the news. Prostration is an expression of reverence. Usually one prostrates before God in worship (see Gen 17:3; Lev 9:24) or before another person out of respect (see Gen 44:14). In Numbers Moses (sometimes with Aaron) is often seen prostrating before God in intercession for the people (see 16:22; 17:10; 20:6). In this passage they fall on their faces before the community (see also 16:4). Is this also intercession for the people or is it an expression of horrified anger? Joshua and Caleb rip their clothes in a traditional sign of grief.

the land, tore their garments ⁷and said to the whole community of the Israelites, "The land which we went through and reconnoitered is an exceedingly good land. ⁸If the LORD is pleased with us, he will bring us in to this land and give it to us, a land which flows with milk and honey. ⁹Only do not rebel against the LORD! You need not be afraid of the people of the land, for they are but food for us! Their protection has left them, but the LORD is with us. Do not fear them."

The Lord's Sentence. ¹⁰The whole community threatened to stone them. But the glory of the LORD appeared at the tent of meeting to all the Israelites. ¹¹And the LORD said to Moses: How long will this people spurn me? How long will they not trust me, despite all the signs I have performed among them? ¹²I will strike them with pestilence and disown them. Then I will make of you a nation greater and mightier than they.

Inserted into this Priestly rendition of the event is a speech of the scouts from the earlier tradition. This speech is put into the mouths of Joshua and Caleb. They plead with the people, repeating their earlier praise of the land (see 13:27). They will be able to take possession of the land not by their own strength but because the Lord is with them. The fierce inhabitants will be helpless because their "protection" has left them. The gods in whom the current inhabitants of Canaan place their trust have deserted them. The Lord will serve the Canaanites up to Israel as a banquet.

14:10-38 The Lord's sentence

The whole community responds in anger, threatening to stone the leaders: Joshua and Caleb and perhaps also Moses and Aaron. They are stopped, however, by the appearance of the Lord's glory at the tent of meeting. The story of the Lord's response to the people's murmuring is told twice, first from an early tradition (14:11-25) and then from the Priestly tradition (14:26-38). In each version the Lord complains "How long!" (14:11, 27) and takes an oath to punish the grumblers, swearing "by my life" (14:21, 28).

In the earlier tradition the Lord decides to wipe out the people and begin again with Moses. (The whole section is remarkably similar to Exod 32–34.) Moses, however, acts as a true prophet. Having pleaded with the people for the sake of God, now he pleads with God for the sake of the people. His argument is simple: "If you destroy this people, Lord, it will ruin your reputation!" He points out that God has been associated publicly with this people ever since the exodus and is still visibly present with them (in Hebrew, revealed "eye to eye") by means of the pillars of cloud and fire. If the Lord wipes them out, the whole world will think that God did not have the power to bring this people into the land promised to them.

¹³But Moses said to the Lord: "The Egyptians will hear of this, for by your power you brought out this people from among them. ¹⁴They will tell the inhabitants of this land, who have heard that you, Lord, are in the midst of this people; you, Lord, who directly revealed yourself! Your cloud stands over them, and you go before them by day in a column of cloud and by night in a column of fire. ¹⁵If now you slay this people all at once, the nations who have heard such reports of you will say, ¹⁶'The Lord was not able to bring this people into the land he swore to give them; that is why he slaughtered them in the wilderness.' ¹⁷Now then, may my Lord's forbearance be great, even as you have said, ¹⁸'The Lord is slow to anger and abounding in kindness, forgiving iniquity and rebellion; yet certainly not declaring the guilty guiltless, but punishing children to the third and fourth generation for their parents' iniquity.' ¹⁹Pardon, then, the iniquity of this people in keeping with your great kindness, even as you have forgiven them from Egypt until now."

²⁰The Lord answered: I pardon them as you have asked. ²¹Yet, by my life and the Lord's glory that fills the whole earth, ²²of all the people who have seen my glory and the signs I did in Egypt and in the wilderness, and who nevertheless have put me to the test ten times already and have not obeyed me, ²³not one shall see the land which I promised on oath to their ancestors. None of those who have spurned me shall see it. ²⁴But as for my servant Caleb, because he has a different spirit and follows me unreservedly, I will bring him into the land which he entered, and his descendants shall possess it. ²⁵But now, since the Amalekites and Canaanites are living in the valleys, turn away tomorrow and set

Moses' second and final argument trumps the first. God has revealed the divine name and nature to this people (see Exod 34:5-7). The Lord is not a God of anger and revenge but of love and forgiveness (Num 14:18). The punishment is limited but God's mercy lasts forever. This statement is Israel's most frequent definition of who God is; it defines the "God of the Old Testament" (see Joel 2:13; Jonah 4:2; Pss 86:15; 103:8; 145:8; Neh 9:17). Moses ends with a plea that God live up to this divine nature and continue to forgive the people.

The Lord submits to Moses' arguments and agrees to pardon the people. This is still a murmuring story, however, and there will be a limited punishment (see chs. 11–12). God swears that all who still refuse to trust in spite of *seeing* the wonderful signs from the exodus onward will never *see* the Promised Land. So Moses is instructed not to travel north toward the Promised Land but to turn south toward the Red Sea in order to circle around Edom and Moab and enter the land from the east. (The Red Sea here probably represents the Gulf of Aqaba/Eilat.) See map on page 154.

out into the wilderness by way of the Red Sea road.

²⁶The Lᴏʀᴅ also said to Moses and Aaron: ²⁷How long will this wicked community grumble against me? I have heard the grumblings of the Israelites against me. ²⁸Tell them: "By my life"—oracle of the Lᴏʀᴅ—"I will do to you just what I have heard you say. ²⁹Here in the wilderness your dead bodies shall fall. Of all your men of twenty years or more, enrolled in your registration, who grumbled against me, ³⁰not one of you shall enter the land where I solemnly swore to settle you, except Caleb, son of Jephunneh, and Joshua, son of Nun. ³¹Your little ones, however, who you said would be taken as spoil, I will bring in, and they shall know the land you rejected. ³²But as for you, your bodies shall fall here in the wilderness, ³³while your children will wander for forty years, suffering for your infidelity, till the last of you lies dead in the wilderness. ³⁴Corresponding to the number of days you spent reconnoitering the land—forty days—you shall bear your punishment one year for each day: forty years. Thus you will realize what it means to oppose me. ³⁵I, the Lᴏʀᴅ, have spoken; and I will surely do this to this entire wicked community that conspired against me: here in the wilderness they shall come to their end and there they will die."

Even Moses is not excused from this judgment. Only the faithful Caleb will be brought into the land. This continual separation of Caleb from the rest of the scouts may be an indication that a small group did succeed in invading from the south (see Num 21:1-3). In the later division of land by Joshua, Caleb is given Hebron (the area he explored) and is reported to have driven out from there the three Anakim mentioned in Numbers 13:22: Sheshai, Ahiman, and Talmai (Josh 15:13-14).

In the Priestly version of the story (vv. 26-38), the Lord complains to both Moses and Aaron. The Lord's oath is a tit-for-tat response to the grumbling of the community: They wished to die in the wilderness (14:2), so everyone registered in the census (see Num 1) will die in the wilderness. Only the children that they feared would be taken captive (14:3) will survive to take possession of the Promised Land. The children, however, will suffer for the sins of their parents. They will be forced to roam the wilderness for forty years—one year for each day of the scouting expedition—until the whole exodus generation has died. This announcement of punishment is sealed by another solemn oath: The Lord has spoken and will do it.

The first to die are the scouts who spoke evil words about the Promised Land. Only Joshua and Caleb are spared. In the earlier tradition Caleb is the one who speaks favorably about the land (13:30) and is the sole survivor of the scouts (14:24); in the Priestly tradition Caleb is joined by Joshua (14:6, 30, 38).

³⁶And the men whom Moses had sent to reconnoiter the land and who on returning had set the whole community grumbling against him by spreading discouraging reports about the land— ³⁷these men who had spread discouraging reports about the land were struck down by the LORD and died. ³⁸Only Joshua, son of Nun, and Caleb, son of Jephunneh, survived of all the men who had gone to reconnoiter the land.

Unsuccessful Invasion. ³⁹When Moses repeated these words to all the Israelites, the people mourned greatly. ⁴⁰Early the next morning they started up high into the hill country, saying, "Here we are, ready to go up to the place that the LORD spoke of: for we did wrong." ⁴¹But Moses said, "Why are you now transgressing the LORD's order? This cannot succeed. ⁴²Do not go up, because the LORD is not in your midst; do not allow yourself to be struck down by your enemies. ⁴³For there the Amalekites and Canaanites will face you, and you will fall by the sword. You have turned back from following the LORD; therefore the LORD will not be with you."

⁴⁴Yet they dared to go up high into the hill country, even though neither the ark of the covenant of the LORD nor Moses left the camp. ⁴⁵And the Amalekites and Canaanites who dwelt in that hill country came down and defeated them, beating them back as far as Hormah.

15 **Secondary Offerings.** ¹The LORD spoke to Moses: ²Speak to the Israelites and say to them: When you enter the land that I am giving you for your settlements, ³if you make to the LORD an oblation from the herd or from the flock—either a burnt offering or a sacrifice, to fulfill a vow, or as a voluntary

14:39-45 Unsuccessful invasion

The earlier tradition picks up the story again to report a further rebellion by the people. They have been told to turn back and make a long journey to enter the land (14:25), but now they regret their murmuring and decide to attempt an invasion of Canaan anyway. Moses warns them that this is not a "Holy War." God, symbolized by the ark of the covenant, is not going with them and neither is Moses. In their stubbornness the people attempt an attack anyway and are soundly defeated. See map on page 154.

15:1-21 Secondary offerings

The purpose of most of this chapter (vv. 1-31) is to supplement the ritual laws given in Leviticus 1–7, adding the ingredients and measurements for the grain and wine offerings that accompany the animal sacrifices. This legislation will apply both to the native-born Israelite and to the resident alien (15:14-16, 26, 29-30). The chapter also provides the story of the scouts with a more hopeful ending. Twice the legislation begins, "When you enter the land" (15:2, 18). God's promise of the land has not been taken away altogether; it has only been delayed.

offering, or for one of your festivals—to produce a pleasing aroma for the LORD, [4]the one presenting the offering shall also present to the LORD a grain offering, a tenth of a measure of bran flour mixed with a fourth of a hin of oil, [5]as well as wine for a libation, a fourth of a hin. You will do this with the burnt offering or the sacrifice, for each lamb. [6]Alternatively for a ram you shall make a grain offering of two tenths of a measure of bran flour mixed with a third of a hin of oil, [7]and for a libation, a third of a hin of wine, thereby presenting a pleasing aroma to the LORD. [8]If you make an offering from the herd—either a burnt offering, or a sacrifice, to fulfill a vow, or as a communion offering to the LORD, [9]with it a grain offering of three tenths of a measure of bran flour mixed with half a hin of oil will be presented; [10]and you will present for a libation, half a hin of wine—a sweet-smelling oblation to the LORD. [11]The same is to be done for each ox, ram, lamb or goat. [12]Whatever the number you offer, do the same for each of them.

[13]All the native-born shall make these offerings in this way, whenever they present a sweet-smelling oblation to the LORD. [14]Likewise, in any future generation, any alien residing with you or anyone else in your midst, who presents an oblation of pleasing aroma to the LORD, must do as you do. [15]There is but one statute for you and for the resident alien, a perpetual statute throughout your generations. You and the resident alien will be alike before the LORD; [16]you and the alien residing with you will have the same rule and the same application of it.

[17]The LORD spoke to Moses: [18]Speak to the Israelites and say to them: When you enter the land into which I am bringing you [19]and eat of the bread of the

---

The first set of sacrifices are burnt offerings, whether whole burnt offerings (see Lev 1:1-17) or the portion burnt for a communion sacrifice, a sacrifice in fulfillment of a vow, or a voluntary offering (See Lev 3:1-17; 7:16). The ingredients and measurements vary with regard to the animal offered:

Figure 5: Measurements of Offerings to Accompany Animal Sacrifice

ANIMAL	FLOUR	OIL	WINE
Sheep or goat	1/10 ephah 2.35 lb.	1/4 hin 1 qt.	1/4 hin 1 qt.
Ram	2/10 ephah 4.7 lb.	1/3 hin 1.35 qts.	1/3 hin 1.35 qts.
Ox	3/10 ephah 7.05. lb.	1/2 hin 2 qts.	1/2 hin 2 qts.

land, you shall offer the LORD a contribution. ²⁰A round loaf from your first batch of dough you shall offer as a contribution. Just like a contribution from the threshing floor you shall offer it. ²¹Throughout your generations you shall give a contribution to the LORD from your first batch of dough.

Purification Offerings. ²²If through inadvertence you fail to do any of these commandments which the LORD has given to Moses—²³anything the LORD commanded you through Moses from the time the LORD first gave the command down through your generations—²⁴if it was done inadvertently without the community's knowledge, the whole community shall sacrifice one bull from the herd as a burnt offering of pleasing aroma to the LORD, along with its prescribed grain offering and libation, as well as one he-goat as a purification offering. ²⁵Then the priest shall make atonement for the whole Israelite community; and they will be forgiven, since it was inadvertence, and for their inadvertence they have brought their offering: an oblation to the LORD as well as their purification offering before the LORD. ²⁶Not only the whole Israelite community but also the aliens residing among you shall be forgiven,

---

An ephah of flour is about 23.5 pounds (2 quarts dry); a hin is just a little more than a gallon. The oil was apparently mixed with the flour or poured over it and the wine poured out as a libation.

In addition, a portion of the first batch of dough is to be offered to God. Paul mentions this practice in the Letter to the Romans: "If the firstfruits are holy, so is the whole batch of dough" (Rom 11:16). This remains a Jewish custom to this day. A small pinch of every batch of dough, about the size of an olive, is burnt in the fire as an offering to God.

15:22-31 Purification offerings

The purpose of this section is similar to that of the previous: the stipulations regarding supplementary offerings to accompany animal sacrifices (15:24). The sacrifices are offered to atone for inadvertent offenses, transgressions committed in ignorance. For example, an individual might eat forbidden food without knowing it was forbidden until later. Even these transgressions must be made right. Anyone, however, who sins willfully and with premeditation (Hebrew: "high-handedly") will not be forgiven. Such a person is to be expelled from the community.

The animals to be sacrificed in this section are different from those required for similar offenses in Leviticus (Lev 4:3-21): here a bull is to be sacrificed as a burnt offering and a goat as a purification offering; in Leviticus the bull is the purification offering. Perhaps this section in Numbers is a further development of the legislation in Leviticus.

since the inadvertent fault affects all the people.

²⁷If it is an individual who sins inadvertently, this person shall bring a yearling she-goat as a purification offering. ²⁸And the priest shall make atonement before the LORD for the one who erred, since the sin was inadvertent, making atonement for the person to secure forgiveness. ²⁹You shall have but one rule for the person who sins inadvertently, whether a native-born Israelite or an alien residing among you.

³⁰But anyone who acts defiantly, whether a native or an alien, reviles the LORD, and shall be cut off from among the people. ³¹For having despised the word of the LORD and broken his commandment, he must be cut off entirely and bear the punishment.

The Sabbath-breaker. ³²While the Israelites were in the wilderness, a man was discovered gathering wood on the sabbath day. ³³Those who caught him at it brought him to Moses and Aaron and the whole community. ³⁴But they put him in custody, for there was no clear decision as to what should be done with him. ³⁵Then the LORD said to Moses: This man shall be put to death; let the whole community stone him outside the camp. ³⁶So the whole community led him outside the camp and stoned him to death, as the LORD had commanded Moses.

Tassels on the Cloak. ³⁷The LORD said to Moses: ³⁸Speak to the Israelites and tell them that throughout their generations they are to make tassels for the corners of their garments, fastening a violet cord to each corner. ³⁹When you use these

15:32-36 The sabbath-breaker

The legislation applying to life in the Promised Land is interrupted by a story of a man gathering wood on the sabbath day. The act of gathering wood may be considered work, which is forbidden on the sabbath (Exod 20:8-11), or the offense may be the intention of making a cooking fire on the sabbath, which is also forbidden (Exod 35:3). The offender is held in custody until the appropriate action can be determined. Since the sabbath law is already clear, the uncertainty must be regarding the type of punishment. Moses is told by the Lord that he should be stoned. The community executes the offender outside the camp according to the Lord's command. Breaking the sabbath is an offense directly against God and is thus a capital crime.

15:37-41 Tassels on the cloak

The final directive in the chapter is the requirement to put blue-violet tassels on the corners of one's garments. This blue-violet is an expensive dye made of a certain kind of snail. It is thus considered precious and associated with royalty and worship. The command is given to "the Israelites" but seems to apply only to men. The purpose of the tassels is to remind the covenant people of their obligation to keep all God's commandments.

tassels, the sight of the cord will remind you of all the commandments of the LORD and you will do them, without prostituting yourself going after the desires of your hearts and your eyes. ⁴⁰Thus you will remember to do all my commandments and you will be holy to your God. ⁴¹I, the LORD, am your God who brought you out of the land of Egypt to be your God: I, the LORD your God.

16 **Rebellion of Korah.** ¹Korah, son of Izhar, son of Kohath, son of Levi, and the Reubenites Dathan and Abiram, sons of Eliab, and On, son of Peleth, son of Reuben took ²two hundred and fifty Israelites who were leaders in the community, members of the council and men of note, and confronted Moses. ³Holding an assembly against Moses and Aaron, they said, "You go too far! The whole community, all of them, are holy; the LORD is in their midst. Why then should you set yourselves over the LORD's assembly?"

⁴When Moses heard this, he fell prostrate. ⁵Then he said to Korah and to all his faction, "May the LORD make known tomorrow morning who belongs to him and who is the holy one and whom he will have draw near to him! The one whom he chooses, he will have draw near to him. ⁶Do this: take your censers, Korah and all his faction, ⁷and put fire in them and place incense in them before

---

Whenever one is tempted to stray, the tassel will remind him to be faithful. God promised in the covenant making that the people would be holy (Exod 19:6); the tassels are a simple means to that end. The directive closes with the opening statement of the commandments: "I, the LORD, am your God who brought you out of the land of Egypt" (15:41; cf. Exod 20:1-2).

16:1-11 Rebellion of Korah

Like chapters 13–14, chapter 16 is two stories woven together: the challenge of Dathan and Abiram concerning Moses' civil leadership from the early tradition (16:1, 12-15, 23-34) and the challenge of Korah and his faction concerning Moses' priestly leadership from the Priestly tradition (16:1-11, 16-22, 35 + ch. 17). The method of weaving the stories together was to insert the name of Korah in the Dathan and Abiram story (16:24, 27, 32) and the names of Dathan and Abiram in the Korah story (16:1).

The story of Korah begins the chapter. Korah is a Kohathite and thus belongs to the most highly respected clan of the Levites. The Kohathites were assigned to care for and carry the sacred objects of the sanctuary: the ark, the veil, the table, the menorah, the altars, and all the other utensils within the tabernacle (Num 3:27-32; 4:1-14). But they have been expressly warned not to touch or even look at these sacred objects until they are wrapped by the priests (4:15-20). Only those who are specifically designated may approach so near to the Holy One and the sacred objects used in worship.

the LORD tomorrow. He whom the LORD then chooses is the holy one. You Levites go too far!"

8Moses also said to Korah, "Hear, now, you Levites! 9Are you not satisfied that the God of Israel has singled you out from the community of Israel, to have you draw near him to maintain the LORD's tabernacle, and to attend upon the community and to serve them? 10He has allowed you and your Levite kins- men with you to approach him, and yet you seek the priesthood too. 11It is therefore against the LORD that you and all your faction are conspiring. As for Aaron, what has he done that you should grumble against him?"

Rebellion of Dathan and Abiram.
12Moses summoned Dathan and Abiram, sons of Eliab, but they answered, "We will not go. 13Are you not satisfied that you have brought us here from a land

---

This limitation is the basis of the challenge against Moses and Aaron. (Moses has functioned primarily as a prophet up to this point, but this challenge has to do with priestly authority.) Korah and his faction declare that the whole community is holy, so why do Moses and Aaron think they have special authority over this ministry? Their argument is soundly based: God did promise to make the people holy if they kept the covenant (Exod 19:6) and the Israelites have just been told to put tassels on their garments so that they will remember to be holy (Num 15:40). But does this holiness mean that they are all called to be priests?

The situation is complicated by the fact that Moses and Aaron are also Kohathites! They are sons of Kohath's son Amram (see Exod 6:18, 20), whereas Korah is a son of Kohath's son Izhar. (According to this genealogy, Korah is the first cousin of Moses and Aaron.) The priesthood, however, has been limited to descendants of Amram, specifically Aaron and his descendants. Is Korah asking, "Who do you think you are?" He says to them, "You go too far!"

Moses responds to this challenge by falling on his face. Is he responding in anger? Or is he prostrating before God asking for help in this tricky situation? In any case, he turns the situation over to God. Korah and his faction are to appear at the tabernacle with censers and incense and the Lord will choose who will draw near to him.

Moses also warns Korah and company: "It is you who go too far!" God has chosen the rest of the Kohathites for a most honorable ministry. Is this not enough? Do they want to be priests too?

16:12-15 Rebellion of Dathan and Abiram

Korah and Aaron both disappear from the scene as a second challenge arises. Moses sends for Dathan and Abiram and they respond, "We will

flowing with milk and honey to have us perish in the wilderness, that now you must also lord it over us? ¹⁴Far from bringing us to a land flowing with milk and honey, or giving us fields and vineyards for our inheritance, will you gouge out our eyes? No, we will not go."

¹⁵Then Moses became very angry and said to the LORD, "Pay no attention to their offering. I have never taken a single donkey from them, nor have I wronged any one of them."

Korah. ¹⁶Moses said to Korah, "You and all your faction shall appear before the LORD tomorrow—you and they and Aaron too. ¹⁷Then each of you take his own censer, put incense in it, and present it before the LORD, two hundred and fifty censers; and you and Aaron, each with his own censer, do the same." ¹⁸So each

---

not go." Their challenge has to do with Moses' civil leadership. They followed him out of Egypt because he told them God had promised them a land flowing with milk and honey. Now they have been told they will die in the wilderness (14:22-23). Looking back, Egypt seems wonderful in their eyes. Egypt is the land of milk and honey, not the Promised Land. As for Moses, he has not only seduced them with false claims, he is also lording it over them.

The argument of Dathan and Abiram fails on two counts. They seem to have forgotten that the reason they will die in the wilderness is their refusal to believe Caleb and go up to enter the Promised Land (13:30–14:4). Second, they are wrong that Moses is flaunting his authority. Moses has been interceding with God for this people from the very moment that they left Egypt (Exod 15:25). When his authority has been challenged, he has prayed for the challengers (Num 12:13). He has begged to be relieved of this burden and has accepted help (Num 11:11-15, 24-29). So Moses is furious with the two because of these false charges and prays that God will not accept their offerings.

16:16-24 Korah

The scene shifts again to Korah and his faction. All of them plus Aaron are to appear at the tent of meeting to offer incense. Each one shall take his censer, gather burning coals from the altar fire, and burn incense. Moses had told Korah and company that the Lord would choose those who would draw near to him. So as they offered the incense, the glory of the Lord appeared to the whole community. Then the Lord makes a choice, telling Moses and Aaron to stand back because the whole community will be consumed by fire. This is the third time God has threatened to destroy the Israelites (see Exod 32:10; Num 14:12). Twice Moses has persuaded God not to do it.

of them took their censers, and laying incense on the fire they had put in them, they took their stand by the entrance of the tent of meeting along with Moses and Aaron. [19]Then, when Korah had assembled all the community against them at the entrance of the tent of meeting, the glory of the LORD appeared to the entire community, [20]and the LORD said to Moses and Aaron: [21]Stand apart from this community, that I may consume them at once. [22]But they fell prostrate and exclaimed, "O God, God of the spirits of all living creatures, if one man sins will you be angry with the whole community?" [23]The LORD answered Moses: [24]Speak to the community and tell them: Withdraw from the area around the tent of Korah, Dathan and Abiram.

Punishment of Dathan and Abiram. [25]Moses, followed by the elders of Israel, arose and went to Dathan and Abiram. [26]Then he spoke to the community, "Move away from the tents of these wicked men and do not touch anything that is theirs: otherwise you too will be swept away because of all their sins." [27]So they withdrew from the area around the tents of Korah, Dathan and Abiram. When Dathan and Abiram had come out and were standing at the entrance of

---

Again Moses and Aaron fall prostrate and beg the Lord not to destroy the whole community. The Priestly interpretation of their plea reflects themes from the period of the Babylonian exile and later. God is appealed to, not as covenant partner with and redeemer of Israel, but as creator of every living thing (see Isa 40:28; 43:15; 45:18). The argument turns on individual responsibility (see Ezek 18): Will God destroy everyone for the sin of one person? Can that be just? This third time the plea of Moses is again effective. God does not destroy the whole people.

16:25-34 Punishment of Dathan and Abiram

This section begins at 16:23. Just as God warned Moses and Aaron to stand back from Korah and company, now God instructs Moses to warn the people to stand back from the tents of Dathan and Abiram. (Note: Aaron has again disappeared and Korah has been inserted into this sentence.) Moses carries out God's command, telling the people not even to touch anything that belongs to these two insurgents. Moses informs Dathan and Abiram that God will decide between them and Moses. If they die an ordinary death at an expected time, then they were right and Moses had usurped authority over them. If the earth opens up and swallows them, however, then God has indeed chosen Moses and Dathan and Abiram are in the wrong. Moses has barely finished his speech when the earth opens and swallows them, their families, and everything they owned. All the people are terrified and flee from this horror.

their tents with their wives, their children, and their little ones, ²⁸Moses said, "This is how you shall know that the LORD sent me to do all I have done, and that it was not of my own devising: ²⁹if these die an ordinary death, merely suffering the fate common to all humanity, the LORD has not sent me. ³⁰But if the LORD makes a chasm, and the ground opens its mouth and swallows them with all belonging to them, and they go down alive to Sheol, then you will know that these men have spurned the LORD." ³¹No sooner had he finished saying all this than the ground beneath them split open, ³²and the earth opened its mouth and swallowed them and their families and all of Korah's people with all their possessions. ³³They went down alive to Sheol with all belonging to them; the earth closed over them, and they disappeared from the assembly. ³⁴But all the Israelites near them fled at their shrieks, saying, "The earth might swallow us too!"

Punishment of Korah. ³⁵And fire from the LORD came forth which consumed the two hundred and fifty men who were offering the incense.

The refusal of Dathan and Abiram to go up when Moses calls may reflect the conflict with the Reubenites (and other Transjordanian tribes) to help the other tribes to take possession of Canaan (see Num 32:1-15). God has promised to "lead them up" out of Egypt into the Promised Land (Exod 3:8, 17; 33:3). At the report of the scouts the people refused to "go up" to the land (Num 13:30-31) and then, too late, went up in rebellion (Num 14:44). In Numbers 32 the Reubenites eventually agree to cross over with the rest of the tribes until they have won the land; then they will return to their good grazing land across the Jordan (Num 32:16-33).

16:35–17:15 Punishment of Korah

Korah (who undoubtedly belongs here in verse 35 rather than in 16:32) and his faction were last seen offering incense at the tent of meeting. Moses and Aaron stepped back when God threatened to consume the whole community. Their prayer saved the community, but not those who were guilty. Fire blazed out from the Lord and consumed Korah and his 250 companions.

The censers and the incense that they used, however, are holy, because they have been offered to God. So Eleazar, who is in charge of all things inside the tabernacle (3:32; 4:16), is summoned to take care of them. He is carefully identified as a son of Aaron, a priest, and so authorized to approach holy things. Eleazar scatters the coals with the incense at some distance away where there is less danger of profanation. Then, in accord with the Lord's instructions, he has the censers hammered into plates to cover the altar. There they will function as a sign (17:3; Hebrew *'oth*) and a reminder (17:5; Hebrew *zikkaron*) that no unauthorized person may attempt to exercise a liturgical role.

17 ¹The Lord said to Moses: ²Tell Eleazar, son of Aaron the priest, to remove the censers from the embers; and scatter the fire some distance away, for they have become holy—³the censers of those who sinned at the cost of their lives. Have them hammered into plates to cover the altar, because in being presented before the Lord they have become holy. In this way they shall serve as a sign to the Israelites. ⁴So taking the bronze censers which had been presented by those who were burned, Eleazar the priest had them hammered into a covering for the altar, ⁵just as the Lord had directed him through Moses. This was to be a reminder to the Israelites that no unauthorized person, no one who was not a descendant of Aaron, should draw near to offer incense before the Lord, lest he meet the fate of Korah and his faction.

⁶The next day the whole Israelite community grumbled against Moses and Aaron, saying, "You have killed the people of the Lord." ⁷But while the community was assembling against them, Moses and Aaron turned toward the tent of meeting, and the cloud now covered it and the glory of the Lord appeared. ⁸Then Moses and Aaron came to the front of the tent of meeting, ⁹and the Lord said to Moses: ¹⁰Remove yourselves from this community, that I may consume them at once. But they fell prostrate.

The language is significant here. In the Priestly tradition covenants are marked by "signs": the covenant with Noah by a rainbow (Gen 9:12-13); the covenant with Abraham by circumcision (Gen 17:11); the Sinai covenant by the sabbath (Exod 31:13, 17). Throughout the Old Testament the wonders that God worked in delivering Israel from Egypt are known as "signs" (e.g., Exod 4:8-9; 10:1-2; Num 14:11, 22; Deut 4:34; 7:19; Pss 78:43; 105:27; 135:9; Neh 9:10). The Passover is called a *zikkaron* (Exod 12:14); liturgical objects such as the ephod worn by Aaron (Exod 28:12) and the trumpets blown to announce festivals also function as a remembrance before the Lord (Num 10:10).

The warning that no unauthorized person (literally "strange man") may approach the altar parallels the story of Nadab and Abihu (Lev 10:1-7). These two sons of Aaron were authorized persons, but they presented unauthorized incense (literally "strange fire"). The Hebrew phrase for "strange man," *ʾish zar*, echoes that for "strange fire," *ʾesh zara*. In liturgical matters anything that is unauthorized is potentially fatal. This is the negative answer to Korah's challenge. Moses has said that God will make known who is chosen to approach the sacred (16:5); the hammered cover on the altar warns that God has not chosen everyone. The positive answer will follow in 17:16-26.

Another murmuring story separates the two responses to Korah's challenge. The pattern is familiar: The whole community grumbles without cause; God is angry and punishes; Moses (through Aaron) intercedes with

¹¹Then Moses said to Aaron, "Take your censer, put fire from the altar in it, lay incense on it, and bring it quickly to the community to make atonement for them; for wrath has come forth from the LORD and the plague has begun." ¹²Aaron took his censer just as Moses directed and ran in among the assembly, where the plague had already begun among the people. Then he offered the incense and made atonement for the people, ¹³while standing there between the living and the dead. And so the scourge was checked. ¹⁴There were fourteen thousand seven hundred dead from the scourge, in addition to those who died because of Korah. ¹⁵When the scourge had been checked, Aaron returned to Moses at the entrance of the tent of meeting.

Aaron's Staff. ¹⁶The LORD now said to Moses: ¹⁷Speak to the Israelites and get from them a staff for each ancestral house,

God; God relents and the punishment ceases. The complaint against Moses and Aaron has to do with the deaths in the previous chapter. The two leaders are seen as murderers. (Ironically, Moses was justly accused of murder in Egypt [Exod 2:11-15], but here he is innocent.) As the community joins together against them, the glory of the Lord appears once more (see 14:10; 16:19). Once more God warns Moses to stand back (16:21; see 16:24, 26). Moses and Aaron, however, prostrate themselves once more before God in intercession (16:22; see 14:5; 16:4).

Moses instructs Aaron to perform his priestly duty to make atonement for the people. Usually atonement rituals require blood, but here Aaron is to do exactly what Korah and his faction did and offer incense (16:6-7); Aaron, however, is authorized to do this and Korah was not. What the Levites were authorized to do was to form a buffer zone between the people and the tabernacle so that a plague would not strike them (Num 8:19). In reaching for priestly status, however, they have failed in their assigned duty. The plague has already begun and some people have died, so Aaron does not hesitate. He *runs* from the tent of meeting into the midst of the people, identifying with them as he makes atonement for them. Through his action the plague is stopped, but not before almost fifteen thousand people have died.

17:16-26 Aaron's staff

The positive response to Korah's challenge follows the murmuring story. Moses has said that God will choose the holy one who may draw near (16:5, 7); now that choice will be made. There is a play on the Hebrew word *matteh*, which can mean either "tribe" or "staff"; the leaders of each ancestral house (i.e., "tribe") will present a "staff." In addition to these twelve staffs, Aaron shall also submit a staff for the house of Levi (17:18, 21). (Levi has not been included in the list of the twelve tribes throughout the book of Numbers;

twelve staffs in all, from all the leaders of their ancestral houses. Write each man's name on his staff; 18and write Aaron's name on Levi's staff. For each head of an ancestral house shall have a staff. 19Then deposit them in the tent of meeting, in front of the covenant, where I meet you. 20The staff of the man whom I choose shall sprout. Thus I will rid myself of the Israelites' grumbling against you.

21So Moses spoke to the Israelites, and all their leaders gave him staffs, twelve in all, one from each leader of their ancestral houses; and Aaron's staff was among them. 22Then Moses deposited the staffs before the LORD in the tent of the covenant. 23The next day, when Moses entered the tent of the covenant, Aaron's staff, representing the house of Levi, had sprouted. It had put forth sprouts, pro-duced blossoms, and borne ripe almonds! 24So Moses brought out all the staffs from the LORD's presence to all the Israelites, and each one identified his own staff and took it. 25Then the LORD said to Moses: Put back Aaron's staff in front of the covenant, for safe keeping as a sign to the rebellious, so that their grumbling against me may cease and they might not die. 26Moses did this. Just as the LORD had commanded him, so he did.

Charge of the Sacred Things. 27Then the Israelites exclaimed to Moses, "We will perish; we are lost, we are all lost! 28Anyone who approaches the tabernacle of the LORD will die! Will there be no end to our perishing?"

18 1The LORD said to Aaron: You and your sons as well as your ancestral house with you shall be responsible

the count has remained twelve because of the division of the tribe of Joseph into Ephraim and Manasseh; see 1:47-54; 2:33.) Whichever staff sprouts will signal God's choice. The choice is first of all between tribes, but there is a suggestion that God will also choose a specific person (17:20).

The thirteen staffs are placed in front of the ark of the covenant, which contains the tablets of the commandments. The very next day Aaron's staff has not only sprouted, but even blossomed and produced almonds! There is now no doubt about the person God has chosen. Aaron's staff lives and the others are dead; just so Aaron may approach the sanctuary, but if un-authorized people do they will die. Moses is to put Aaron's staff in front of the ark as a sign (Hebrew *'oth*) to warn the people so that their grumbling will cease. Later tradition will include Aaron's rod as one of the objects kept within the ark of the covenant (Heb 9:4).

Korah's clan does not disappear altogether. In later tradition the Ko-rahites are recognized as singers (2 Chr 20:19; Pss 42, 44–49; 84–85) and as gatekeepers for the temple (1 Chr 9:19; 26:1).

17:27–18:7 Charge of the sacred things

The people have finally gotten the point, but their response shows a typical exaggeration. Now they are terrified that they will all die because

for any sin with respect to the sanctuary; but only you and your sons with you shall be responsible for any sin with respect to your priesthood. ²You shall also present with you your kinsmen of the tribe of Levi, your ancestral tribe, that they may be joined to you and assist you, while you and your sons with you are in front of the tent of the covenant. ³They shall discharge your obligations and those with respect to the whole tent; however, they shall not come near the utensils of the sanctuary or the altar, or else both they and you will die. ⁴They will be joined to you to perform the duties associated with the tent of meeting, all the labor pertaining to the tent. But no unauthorized person shall come near you. ⁵You shall perform the duties of the sanctuary and of the altar, that wrath may not fall again upon the Israelites.

⁶I hereby take your kinsmen, the Levites, from among the Israelites; they are a gift to you, dedicated to the Lord for the labor they perform for the tent of meeting. ⁷But you and your sons with you must take care to exercise your priesthood in whatever concerns the altar and the area within the veil. I give you your priesthood as a gift. Any unauthorized person who comes near shall be put to death.

The Priests' Share of the Sacrifices. ⁸The Lord said to Aaron: I hereby give

---

they have seen Aaron's staff, which is now holy. The section that began with Korah's challenge that, since all the people are holy, they should all be allowed to touch holy things and exercise sacred ministry, ends with the people's terror in the presence of the holy.

In order to alleviate the people's fear the Lord gives Aaron instructions regarding the boundaries of the sanctuary. The Lord usually speaks to Moses but, outside of this chapter (18:1, 8, 20), speaks to Aaron only one other time (Lev 10:8). All of these passages treat the prerogatives of the priesthood and the danger of improperly approaching God.

Aaron is told that from now on he and the whole house of Levi will be responsible for the sin of anyone who crosses the sacred boundaries; they must guard the sanctuary or they will bear the punishment. Aaron and his sons, the priests, are responsible for all ministry within the sanctuary as well as the purity of the priesthood. The other Levites will maintain and guard the tent of meeting and serve the priests who minister there. Each group has its own duties and its own boundaries. No one, including Levites, may usurp the prerogatives of the priests; none of the other Israelites may usurp the prerogatives of the Levites.

18:8-20 The priests' share of the sacrifices

The priests are given no inheritance in the land; God is their heritage. But they must have some compensation for their ministry in order to survive.

to you charge of the contributions made to me, including the various holy offerings of the Israelites; I assign them to you and to your sons as a perquisite, a perpetual due. ⁹This is what you shall have from the oblations that are most holy: every offering of theirs—namely, all their grain offerings, purification offerings, and reparation offerings which they must return to me—shall be most holy for you and for your sons. ¹⁰You shall eat them in a most holy place; every male may partake of them. As holy, they belong to you.

¹¹This also you shall have: the contributions that are their gifts, including the elevated offering of the Israelites; I assign them to you and to your sons and

---

Thus they are given a share in all the sacrifices and offerings at the sanctuary except holocausts, which are totally consumed by fire. A distinction must be made, however, between the "most holy" oblations and other offerings. The "most holy" offerings include the grain offerings, purification offerings, and reparation offerings (see Lev 6:7–7:10). Only a portion of each of these offerings is burned. The rest may be eaten only by ritually clean priests and only within the precincts of the sanctuary. The various kinds of communion sacrifices—the thanksgiving sacrifice, the free-will offering, the sacrifice in fulfillment of a vow— however, are divided differently. The portion that is given to the Lord may be eaten not only by the priests, but by anyone in their families who is ritually clean; the rest of the sacrifice is eaten by the offerer and those to whom he gives it (see Lev 7:11-21). The same is to be done for elevated offerings (see Lev 7:28-36). In addition the priests and their families may have the best (literally "fat") of grain and wine and oil as well as first fruits, which the Israelites donate to the sanctuary (see Deut 18:4; 26:2).

Two other occasions provide contributions for the priests and their families. First, whatever is put under the ban (Hebrew *herem*) is to be given to them (18:14). *Herem* means that everything is set aside for God: spoils of war (including prisoners), property of those condemned to death, or any other condemned or dedicated property. In this chapter the ban applies primarily to hereditary land or any goods that someone has vowed to dedicate to the Lord (see Lev 27:21, 28; Num 30:2-17) or the property of those condemned to death (see Exod 22:19; Lev 27:29). (See commentary on Num 31 regarding the ban applied to spoils of war.)

Second, the firstborn that belong to the Lord are to be given to the priests. Firstborn sons and animals unfit for sacrifice are redeemed with money; firstborn of clean animals must be sacrificed. Both the money and the meat belong to the priests.

daughters with you as a perpetual due. All in your household who are clean may eat them. ¹²I also assign to you all the best of the new oil and of the new wine and grain that they give to the LORD as their first produce that has been processed. ¹³The first-ripened fruits of whatever is in their land, which they bring to the LORD, shall be yours; all of your household who are clean may eat them. ¹⁴Whatever is under the ban in Israel shall be yours. ¹⁵Every living thing that opens the womb, human being and beast alike, such as are to be offered to the LORD, shall be yours; but you must redeem the firstborn of human beings, as well as redeem the firstborn of unclean animals. ¹⁶For the redemption price of a son, when he is a month old, you shall pay the equivalent of five silver shekels according to the sanctuary shekel, that is, twenty gerahs. ¹⁷But the firstborn of cattle, or the firstborn of sheep or the firstborn of goats you shall not redeem; they are holy. Their blood you must splash on the altar and their fat you must burn as an oblation of pleasing aroma to the LORD. ¹⁸Their meat, however, shall be yours, just as the brisket of the elevated offering and the right thigh belong to you. ¹⁹As a perpetual due I assign to you and to your sons and daughters with you all the contributions of holy things which the Israelites set aside for the LORD; this is a covenant of salt to last forever before the LORD, for you and for your descendants with you. ²⁰Then the LORD said to Aaron: You shall not have any heritage in their land nor hold any portion among them; I will be your portion and your heritage among the Israelites.

Tithes Due the Levites. ²¹To the Levites, however, I hereby assign all tithes in Israel as their heritage in recompense for the labor they perform, the labor pertaining to the tent of meeting. ²²The Israelites may no longer approach the tent

---

These stipulations for the upkeep of the priests are sealed in a covenant of salt. This designation presumably refers to the stipulation of offering salt with sacrifice (Lev 2:13; Ezek 43:24) and the custom of eating salt together as a symbol of permanent bonding (Ezra 4:14; 2 Chr 13:5; Mark 9:50).

18:21-24 Tithes due the Levites

The Levites, like the priests, inherit no land and need compensation for their services at the tent of meeting. The Israelites are reminded that the Levites protect them from the dangerous holiness of God in the sanctuary. Thus they have been assigned all the tithes that the Israelites must give to the Lord. Tithing is not voluntary in Israel; it is a kind of tax due to the Lord. The people are to give a tenth of all the produce of their land: the fields, vineyards, and orchards. (Legislation regarding tithes is not consistent; compare Deut 12:17-19; 14:22-29). Anyone who wishes to pay a tithe in money instead of produce must give an additional twenty percent (see Lev 27:30-31).

of meeting, thereby incurring the penalty of death. ²³Only the Levites are to perform the labor pertaining to the tent of meeting, and they shall incur the penalty for the Israelites' sin; this is a permanent statute for all your generations. But they shall not have any heritage among the Israelites, ²⁴for I have assigned to the Levites as their heritage the tithes which the Israelites put aside as a contribution to the LORD. That is why I have said, they will not have any heritage among the Israelites.

Tithes Paid by the Levites. ²⁵The LORD said to Moses: ²⁶Speak to the Levites and say to them: When you take from the Israelites the tithes I have assigned you from them as your heritage, you are to make a contribution from them to the LORD, a tithe of the tithe; ²⁷and your contribution will be credited to you as if it were grain from the threshing floor or new wine from the vat.

²⁸Thus you too shall make a contribution to the LORD from all the tithes you take from the Israelites, handing over to Aaron the priest the contribution to the LORD. ²⁹From all the gifts to you, you shall make every contribution due to the LORD—from their best parts, that is the part to be consecrated from them.

³⁰Say to them also: Once you have made your contribution from the best part, the rest of the tithe will be credited to the Levites as if it were produce of the threshing floor or the produce of the vat. ³¹You and your households may eat it anywhere, since it is your recompense in exchange for labor in the tent of meeting. ³²You will incur no punishment when you contribute the best part of it. But do not profane the holy offerings of the Israelites or else you shall die.

19 Ashes of the Red Heifer. ¹The LORD spoke to Moses and Aaron: ²This is the statute for the ritual which

---

18:25-32 Tithes paid by the Levites

The Levites in their turn must also pay a tithe to the priests. Since they have no land and thus cannot give the regular tithe to the priesthood, they are required to give one-tenth to the priests from all the tithes that they receive. This tithe frees them to do what they wish with the other nine-tenths. The produce and money that the Israelites have given them were dedicated to the Lord, but once the Levites pay their own tithe from this offering, the rest is no longer sacred. They may consume it with their families just as the rest of the Israelites consume the rest of the produce from their land.

19:1-10 Ashes of the red heifer

The legislation regarding purification from contamination by a corpse is intense and unique. Every other legislation regarding purification involves at least some ritual action at the sanctuary; the ritual preparation of this purification water, however, takes place not only outside the sanctuary but even outside the camp. All those who are involved in the preparation of this water of purification are defiled by the ritual; nowhere else is a priest said to

the LORD has commanded. Tell the Israelites to procure for you a red heifer without defect and free from every blemish and on which no yoke has ever been laid. ³You will give it to Eleazar the priest, and it will be led outside the camp and slaughtered in his presence. ⁴Eleazar the priest will take some of its blood on his finger and sprinkle it seven times toward the front of the tent of meeting. ⁵Then the heifer will be burned in his sight; it will be burned with its hide and flesh, its blood and dung; ⁶and the priest will take cedar wood, hyssop and scarlet yarn and throw them into the fire in which the heifer is being burned. ⁷The priest shall then wash his garments and bathe his body in water, afterward

---

be defiled as a result of ritual action. Contamination by a corpse threatens to defile not only the person involved, but even the tabernacle itself.

The preparation of the water begins with the acquisition of the proper animal: a red cow who has no defects and who has never been used for ordinary work. Even though virtually every translation identifies this animal as a "heifer" (i.e., a young cow who has never borne a calf), the Hebrew word is the ordinary word for "cow" (*parah*). The cow must be red, probably to symbolize blood. Blood is a powerful agent for purification. The cow must never have been used as a draft animal. An animal offered to God should not have been previously used for human purposes. The same stipulation is required of the two cows (who have borne calves) that in Samuel's time bring the ark home from the Philistines (1 Sam 6:7).

Eleazar the priest supervises the ritual. Eleazar is rising to prominence at this point in the story. Aaron's eldest sons, Nadab and Abihu, died after offering unauthorized incense (Lev 10:1-2). Eleazar is next in line and will succeed Aaron. He has already been put in charge of everything within the sanctuary (Num 3:32; 4:16). It is he who scattered the coals and incense after the incident with Korah and who had the censers hammered into a covering for the altar (17:1-3).

Eleazar's role in this ritual is central but limited. He takes the blood of the slaughtered cow and sprinkles it seven times toward the tent of meeting. The tent, which here is understood to be in the center of the camp, is at some distance from the action that takes place outside the camp. Nevertheless, since it is threatened with defilement, it must be included symbolically in the purification. Sprinkling blood seven times is part of the ritual in the standard purification offerings (Lev 4:6, 17), on the Day of Atonement (Lev 16:14, 19), and for the cleansing of those suffering from skin disease (Lev 14:7, 27; cf. 14:51). The whole cow is burned, including its blood. The burned blood in the ashes of the cow will still have power to purify.

he may enter the camp. The priest remains unclean until the evening. ⁸Likewise, the one who burned the heifer shall wash his garments in water, bathe his body in water, and be unclean until evening. ⁹Then somebody who is clean shall gather up the ashes of the heifer and deposit them in a clean place outside the camp. There they are to be kept to prepare purification water for the Israelite community. This is a purification offering. ¹⁰The one who has gathered up the ashes of the heifer shall also wash his garments and be unclean until evening. This is a permanent statute, both for the Israelites and for the alien residing among them.

Use of the Ashes. ¹¹Those who touch the corpse of any human being will be unclean for seven days; ¹²they shall purify themselves with the water on the third and on the seventh day, and then

---

While the cow is being burned, Eleazar throws cedar, hyssop, and scarlet yarn in the fire. The cedar is used no doubt because of its aromatic properties. Hyssop, also highly aromatic, is used twice in the ritual: it is burned with the cow and its branches are used to sprinkle the water. The scarlet yarn may also symbolize blood. The same three elements are used with blood in the ritual to purify someone who has been healed of skin disease (Lev 14:4, 6; cf. 14:49-52). "Cleanse me with hyssop, that I may be pure" (Ps 51:9) is a reminder of these purification rituals.

Several men assist Eleazar. Someone brings the red cow and slaughters it in Eleazar's presence. Someone burns the red cow; someone who is ritually clean gathers up the ashes of the cow and puts them in a place outside the camp where they will not be defiled. The priest and the one who burned the cow are unclean and must bathe and wash their clothes. The one who gathers the ashes is also unclean, but apparently less so. He is only required to wash his clothes. They all remain unclean until evening.

19:11-22 Use of the ashes

These ashes of the red cow, which have been so carefully prepared, must be mixed with living water, that is, water flowing from a spring or other source. The resulting "purification water" is to be used to purify someone who is unclean because of having touched the dead body of a human being. A human corpse is regarded as having the potential for powerful contamination. If someone dies in an enclosed space, a tent or building, everything within the tent and everyone who is in the tent or enters it is unclean for seven days. The only things that are protected are things in closed pots. The contamination is somewhat less severe out in the open. Only the person who touches the dead body is unclean for seven days. In either case, however, everything and everyone that the unclean person touches also

81

be clean. But if they fail to purify themselves on the third and on the seventh day, they will not become clean. [13]Those who touch the corpse of a human being who dies and who fail to purify themselves defile the tabernacle of the LORD and these persons shall be cut off from Israel. Since the purification water has not been splashed over them, they remain unclean: their uncleanness is still on them.

[14]This is the ritual: When someone dies in a tent, everyone who enters the tent, as well as everyone already in it, will be unclean for seven days; [15]and every open vessel with its lid unfastened will be unclean. [16]Moreover, everyone who in the open country touches a person who has been slain by the sword or who has died naturally, or who touches a human bone or a grave, will be unclean for seven days. [17]For anyone who is thus unclean, ashes shall be taken from the burnt purification offering, and spring water will be poured on them from a vessel. [18]Then someone who is clean will take hyssop, dip it in this water, and sprinkle it on the tent and on all the vessels and persons that were in it, or on the one who touched the bone, the slain person or the other

becomes unclean. Even the person who sprinkles the purification water is also rendered unclean until evening.

The person made unclean by contact with a dead body must be cleansed by the purification water. On the third and seventh day this water is to be sprinkled on him or her by someone ritually clean (not a priest). The same water must be sprinkled on whatever object has become unclean. After the seventh day the unclean person must bathe and wash clothes and will then be declared clean. This process is absolutely necessary. Twice it is stated that anyone who fails to submit to this ritual of purification remains unclean forever and will be cut off from the community. Otherwise the person's very presence in the camp would defile the Lord's sanctuary.

The purpose of this ritual is not simply hygienic. According to this legislation even the bone of a person long dead or a grave renders someone unclean. The purpose therefore must be sought somewhere else. There is a strong resistance in ancient Israel to anything suggesting worship of the dead. Ancestors are remembered, but they are not to be consulted about future actions (Lev 19:31; 20:6, 27; Deut 18:11; 2 Kgs 21:6; 23:24; Isa 8:19). Saul forbade the summoning of the dead by necromancers; when he was in desperate straits and asked the medium in Endor to call up Samuel, Samuel's response is to scold him (1 Sam 28:7-20; see 1 Chr 10:13). Manasseh, regarded as Judah's most wicked king, consulted the dead (2 Kgs 21:6; 2 Chr 33:6); his grandson Josiah "purged the consultation of ghosts and spirits, with the household gods, idols, and all the other horrors to be seen in the land of Judah and in Jerusalem" (2 Kgs 23:24).

corpse, or the grave. ¹⁹The clean will sprinkle the unclean on the third and on the seventh day, and thus purify them on the seventh day. Then they will wash their garments and bathe in water, and in the evening be clean. ²⁰Those who become unclean and fail to purify themselves—those people will be cut off from the assembly, because they defile the sanctuary of the LORD. The purification water has not been splashed over them; they remain unclean. ²¹This will be a permanent statute for you.

Those who sprinkle the purification water will wash their garments, and those who come in contact with the purification water will be unclean until evening. ²²Moreover, anything that the unclean person touches becomes unclean itself, and the one who touches such a person becomes unclean until evening.

20 **Death of Miriam.** ¹The Israelites, the whole community, arrived in the wilderness of Zin in the first month, and the people stayed at Kadesh. It was here that Miriam died, and here that she was buried.

Need for Water at Kadesh. ²Since the community had no water, they held an assembly against Moses and Aaron. ³The

---

Most of the peoples in the ancient Near East from Egypt to Mesopotamia had a cult of the dead. God's covenant people are not allowed to succumb to this practice. Declaring a dead body to be a powerful source of uncleanness is a deterrent against turning to the dead person for advice and assistance. It is a short step from consulting the dead and asking them for help to worshiping them. Israel is to look to God who leads them into the future rather than depending on the dead who are buried in the past.

20:1 Death of Miriam

Chapter 20 signals the end of the wilderness period. Miriam dies in the first verse; Moses and Aaron are informed in verse 12 that they will die before the entrance into the land. Aaron dies in verse 28. The exodus generation has been told they will all die in the wilderness; this warning indicates these three major leaders of the community will die with the rest of their generation. Miriam's death is reported simply with no comment about mourning.

Because of the interweaving of traditions there is some confusion in the geography. The Priestly tradition seems to indicate that the people have just arrived at Kadesh, whereas the earlier tradition located them at Kadesh already when the scouts went up to spy out the land (13:26). The same inconsistency is probably the reason no year is mentioned in this verse. Later Aaron's death is dated to the fortieth year after the departure from Egypt (33:38).

20:2-6a Need for water at Kadesh

Again the people complain. This story, however, is not like the other murmuring stories in Numbers. This story follows the pattern seen in

people quarreled with Moses, exclaiming, "Would that we had perished when our kindred perished before the Lord! ⁴Why have you brought the Lord's assembly into this wilderness for us and our livestock to die here? ⁵Why have you brought us up out of Egypt, only to bring us to this wretched place? It is not a place for grain nor figs nor vines nor pomegranates! And there is no water to drink!" ⁶But Moses and Aaron went away from the assembly to the entrance of the tent of meeting, where they fell prostrate.

Sin of Moses and Aaron. Then the glory of the Lord appeared to them,

Exodus: the people have a genuine need; they murmur; Moses prays; God provides. This is the first murmuring story in Numbers where there is a genuine need; it is the Priestly parallel to the earlier water story in Exodus 17. The people's complaint looks like mutiny; they hold an assembly against Moses and Aaron. They bemoan the fact that they did *not* perish in their previous episodes of murmuring: in their desire for meat (Num 11:33), in their refusal to believe Caleb's report (Num 14:11-20), in their rebellion against the leadership of Moses and Aaron (Num 17:6-15; see 17:27-28). They repeat the now-familiar refrain: "Why have you brought us out of Egypt?" The wilderness is no land of promise! The inclusion of Aaron as a leader along with Moses identifies the source of this story as the Priestly tradition. Both of them hear the complaint and fall prostrate in petition at the tent of meeting. The final element in the pattern, God's response to the people's need, follows in the next section.

20:6b-13 Sin of Moses and Aaron

Once more the glory of the Lord appears at a critical moment (see 14:10; 16:19; 17:7). The Lord gives Moses instructions to provide the people with the needed water. He is to take the staff—his or Aaron's that is in the tent of meeting—and command the rock to give water. An abundance of water will pour forth at his word alone. The Lord is not angry as in the other murmuring stories in Numbers because now the people have expressed a genuine need. Moses, however, *is* angry. First, he scolds the people, calling them rebels and suggesting that they are unworthy of having water come from the rock for them. Then, instead of commanding the rock to yield water, he strikes it not once but twice.

God keeps his part of the bargain; the water gushes out in abundance and the people are satisfied. But Moses and Aaron do not get off so easily. (Aaron is complicit in the failure simply by his presence; he does not escape here as he did in the incident with Miriam in ch. 12.) These two

A Bedoin desert tent

⁷and the Lord said to Moses: ⁸Take the staff and assemble the community, you and Aaron your brother, and in their presence command the rock to yield its waters. Thereby you will bring forth water from the rock for them, and supply the community and their livestock with water. ⁹So Moses took the staff from its place before the Lord, as he was ordered. ¹⁰Then Moses and Aaron gathered the assembly in front of the rock, where he said to them, "Just listen, you rebels! Are we to produce water for you out of this rock?" ¹¹Then, raising his hand, Moses struck the rock twice with his staff, and water came out in abundance, and the community and their livestock drank. ¹²But the Lord said to Moses and Aaron: Because you did not have confidence in me, to acknowledge my holiness before the Israelites, therefore you shall not lead this assembly into the land I have given them.

¹³These are the waters of Meribah, where the Israelites quarreled with the Lord, and through which he displayed his holiness.

Edom's Refusal. ¹⁴From Kadesh Moses sent messengers to the king of Edom: "Thus says your brother Israel:

---

leaders neither followed God's command nor imitated God's generosity to the people. They did not trust God's goodness. Thus they have not demonstrated God's holiness to the people. Therefore they too will die in the wilderness with the rest of their generation.

Other attempts are made to explain the reason that Moses and Aaron are prevented from entering the Promised Land. In Psalm 106 the people are blamed (Ps 106:32-33; see Deut 1:37; 3:26; 4:21-22). Some interpreters say they are punished because Moses struck the rock twice instead of once; however, Moses was not told to strike the rock at all. He was told just to speak to the rock. Other commentators point out that from the exodus generation only Caleb and Joshua are permitted to enter the land (14:21-24, 29-30). Whatever the reason, it is clear from this chapter that a new generation will pioneer in the land God promised to their ancestors.

The passage ends, as most of the murmuring stories do, with an explanation of the place names: "Meribah" is derived from the Hebrew word *rib*, which means "to contend against." The name "Kadesh" is suggested by the comment that there God displayed divine holiness (Hebrew *yiqqadesh*).

20:14-21 Edom's refusal

In the earlier tradition, after the Israelites refused to go up to the land at Caleb's urging, God told them two things: first, the whole adult generation would die in the wilderness; and second, they would not enter Canaan from the south but would go back to the Red Sea (probably here

You know of all the hardships that have befallen us, ¹⁵how our ancestors went down to Egypt, and we stayed in Egypt a long time, and the Egyptians treated us and our ancestors harshly. ¹⁶When we cried to the LORD, he heard our cry and sent an angel who led us out of Egypt. Now here we are at Kadesh, a town at the edge of your territory. ¹⁷Please let us pass through your land. We will not cross any fields or vineyards, nor drink any well water, but we will go straight along the King's Highway without turn-ing to the right or to the left, until we have passed through your territory."

¹⁸But Edom answered him, "You shall not pass through here; if you do, I will advance against you with the sword." ¹⁹The Israelites said to him, "We will go up along the highway. If we or our live-stock drink any of your water, we will pay for it. It is nothing—just let us pass through on foot." ²⁰But Edom replied, "You shall not pass through," and ad-vanced against them with a large and heavily armed force. ²¹Therefore, since

the Gulf of Aqaba) and come around to enter from the east (14:25). Thus Moses sends messengers to the king of Edom to gain permission to travel through his land toward the eastern side of the Dead Sea. His appeal to Edom as a brother is not without merit. Edom is another name for Esau, just as Israel is another name for Jacob (Gen 25:30; 32:29; 35:10). The twin sons of Isaac and Rebekah are believed to be the ancestors of the Edomites and the Israelites.

Moses reports to the Edomite king the whole story from Jacob's going down into Egypt to their arrival back at the borders of Edom. He tells how God sent an angel to deliver them from Egyptian persecution and slavery (see Exod 14:19; 23:20-23; 32:34). Now Moses has sent a messenger to the king of Edom. (In Hebrew the same word is translated both "messenger" and "angel.") Then Moses makes his request: "Please let us pass through your land" (20:17). He promises they will take absolutely nothing. The King's Highway is an ancient caravan route, stretching from the Red Sea (modern Gulf of Aqaba) to Damascus. It passes through Edom and runs up the eastern side of the Dead Sea and the Jordan valley. Traces of it, rebuilt by the Romans, can still be seen today. See map on page 155.

The king of Edom refuses, threatening violence against the Israelites if they cross their borders. Even when the Israelites insist, Edom rejects their request. So the Israelites turn back to go all the way around Edom's south-ern and eastern borders. Deuteronomy tells the story somewhat differently. The Israelites pass through Edom and Moab, but the Amorite king, Sihon, refuses to let them pass (see Num 21:21-35). Israel's attack against him is the first battle of the entry into the land (Deut 2; see Num 21).

Edom refused to let Israel pass through their territory, Israel turned away from them.

Death of Aaron. ²²Setting out from Kadesh, the Israelites, the whole community, came to Mount Hor. ²³There at Mount Hor, on the border of the land of Edom, the LORD said to Moses and Aaron: ²⁴Let Aaron be gathered to his people, for he shall not enter the land I have given to the Israelites, because you both rebelled against my directions at the waters of Meribah. ²⁵Take Aaron and Eleazar his son and bring them up on Mount Hor. ²⁶Then strip Aaron of his garments and put them on Eleazar, his son; but there Aaron shall be gathered up in death.

²⁷Moses did as the LORD commanded. When they had climbed Mount Hor in view of the whole community, ²⁸Moses stripped Aaron of his garments and put them on Eleazar his son. Then Aaron died there on top of the mountain. When Moses and Eleazar came down from the mountain, ²⁹all the community understood that Aaron had breathed his last; and for thirty days the whole house of Israel mourned Aaron.

21 Victory over Arad. ¹When the Canaanite, the king of Arad, who

20:22-29 Death of Aaron

Miriam died at the beginning of this chapter; Aaron dies at the end. Much more attention is given to his death, however. The Israelites have traveled some distance along the Edomite border to Mount Hor, an unidentified location; the name "Hor" means "the mountain." Aaron and his son Eleazar are to be brought up this (small?) mountain and to perform the ritual transfer of authority in the sight of all the people. The priestly vestments are taken off Aaron and put on Eleazar, who thus assumes the office of high priest (see Lev 8:7-9). When this is accomplished Aaron dies; only Moses and Eleazar descend from the mountain. The community mourns for thirty days, much longer than the traditional seven-day period (see 1 Sam 31:13; Jdt 16:24; Sir 22:11). Deuteronomy reports that the mourning period for Moses was also thirty days (Deut 34:8). The Egyptians mourned Jacob for seventy days, but Joseph later observed the traditional seven days of mourning (Gen 50:3, 10).

21:1-3 Victory over Arad

This puzzling little passage seems the direct opposite of the Israelites' earlier experience at Hormah (14:39-45). At that time they had refused to go up and take possession of the land in spite of Caleb's advice. After God declared that they would indeed die in the wilderness as they had asked, they attempted to attack even though Moses warned that God would not go with them. In that event they were soundly defeated. Now, only a short time later, they are attacked by the king of Arad (in the southern Negeb near Hormah) and some Israelites are taken captive. They plan to attack but

ruled over the Negeb, heard that the Israelites were coming along the way of Atharim, he engaged Israel in battle and took some of them captive. ²Israel then made this vow to the LORD: "If you deliver this people into my hand, I will put their cities under the ban." ³The LORD paid attention to Israel and delivered up the Canaanites, and they put them and their cities under the ban. Hence that place was named Hormah.

---

they also promise God that they will abide by the customs of holy war: (1) they will recognize that the victory is won by God's power, not their own; (2) they will not enrich themselves with plunder but will dedicate it all to God. As a result, they are victorious.

The first principle of holy war is based on the exodus experience. Pharaoh pursues the fleeing Israelites, who are unarmed, with all his chariots and horses. The victory clearly belongs to God (Exod 14:13-14). Throughout the Old Testament there is a consistent warning not to trust in armaments (horses and chariots) or in the size of the army, but to trust in God (see Judg 7:1-7; Ps 20:8-9; Isa 31:1; Mic 5:9-12).

This second principle is called *herem* in Hebrew and is translated either as "the ban" or "doom." War must not be waged for profit. God wins the victory; the spoils belong to God. Either all the plunder is destroyed—all living beings killed and all property burned (Deut 2:34; Josh 6:18, 21)—or some of it is offered to God at the sanctuary (Lev 27:21; Num 18:14).

This story of victory in Canaan seems out of place here; a more likely victory at Hormah is reported in Judges 1:17. The next passage about the bronze serpent (21:4-9) seems to follow directly from chapter 20 with the departure from Mount Hor; the story of Hormah looks like an insertion. There are two possible reasons for this anticipation of the entrance into the Promised Land. First of all, Caleb was exempted from God's decision that the exodus generation would all die in the wilderness (14:24). This story may explain the report in Joshua that Caleb holds the territory in the southern Negeb (Josh 14:13-14; Judg 1:12-15; 1 Sam 30:14). Second, this story, taken with the earlier failed attempt to enter Canaan from the south, may illustrate the way by which Israel should take possession of the Promised Land. This second experience in the southern Negeb, in contrast to the first attempt, results in victory. In the first attempt the people act on their own in disobedience to God and they fail. In this second attempt they trust God to give them the victory and they subsequently give both the credit and the spoils to God. The place is named (again) "Hormah," a word that suggests the practice of *herem* (see 14:45).

The Bronze Serpent. [4]From Mount Hor they set out by way of the Red Sea, to bypass the land of Edom, but the people's patience was worn out by the journey; [5]so the people complained against God and Moses, "Why have you brought us up from Egypt to die in the wilderness, where there is no food or water? We are disgusted with this wretched food!"

[6]So the LORD sent among the people seraph serpents, which bit the people so that many of the Israelites died. [7]Then the people came to Moses and said, "We have sinned in complaining against the LORD and you. Pray to the LORD to take the serpents from us." So Moses prayed for the people, [8]and the LORD said to Moses: Make a seraph and mount it on a pole, and everyone who has been bit-

21:4-9 The bronze serpent

Following God's instructions (14:25), the Israelites set out by way of the Red Sea road to go around Edom. But before they leave the wilderness there must be one more murmuring story. This story is like all the murmuring stories in Numbers (except the grumbling about water in chapter 20): the people's complaint again seems unfounded. They claim there is no food or water, yet they are disgusted with the food they have. As usual, when there is grumbling without cause, God grows angry and punishes the people. Moses then prays and God relents.

The punishment is in the form of "seraph serpents." *Saraph* in Hebrew means "burning." Perhaps this name refers to the poisonous (thus burning) bite of the serpents. In Isaiah 14:29 and 30:6 *seraphim* (plural of *saraph*) are clearly serpents, associated with vipers and adders, and they also fly. *Seraphim* appear once more in Isaiah during his call vision (6:2, 6). The six-winged *seraphim* hover aloft and cry out, "Holy, holy, holy is the LORD of hosts." One of them brings a *burning* coal to cleanse the prophet's lips. Seraphim in Isaiah's vision seem to be guardians of God's throne. They may be modeled on the hooded cobra, a sacred animal in Egypt imaged even on the pharaoh's headdress.

God instructs Moses to provide for the people's healing with a kind of sympathetic magic. He is to mount a bronze *saraph* on a pole, and anyone who looks at it will live. The *saraph* serpent thus becomes associated with healing as well as with death. This ambiguous meaning of the serpent as a symbol is found throughout the ancient world and still today. Moses' own staff was turned into a serpent (Exod 4:3; 7:15). In the eighth century Hezekiah removes a bronze serpent from the temple because apparently it had become a temptation to idolatry (2 Kgs 18:4). The serpent in Genesis 3 becomes in later tradition a symbol for the devil (see Wis 2:24). In the Gospel

ten will look at it and recover. ⁹Accordingly Moses made a bronze serpent and mounted it on a pole, and whenever the serpent bit someone, the person looked at the bronze serpent and recovered.

Journey Around Moab. ¹⁰The Israelites moved on and encamped in Oboth. ¹¹Then they moved on from Oboth and encamped in Iye-abarim in the wilderness facing Moab on the east. ¹²Moving on from there, they encamped in the Wadi Zered. ¹³Moving on from there, they encamped on the other side of the Arnon, in the wilderness that extends from the territory of the Amorites; for the Arnon forms Moab's boundary, between Moab and the Amorites. ¹⁴Hence it is said in the "Book of the Wars of the LORD":

> "Waheb in Suphah and the wadies,
> ¹⁵Arnon and the wadi gorges
> That reach back toward the site of Ar
> and lean against the border of Moab."

---

of John the evangelist sees the raised serpent as a type of Christ on the cross (John 3:14-15). Today the symbol of medicine, the caduceus, consists of serpents entwined around a winged staff.

21:10-20 Journey around Moab

The story of the bronze serpent marks the transition from the wilderness wandering to the purposeful movement toward the Promised Land. The Israelites have journeyed around Edom and rapidly move around Moab. Most of this section is a simple listing of places. The first two camping sites mentioned in this brief itinerary are unknown: the name "Oboth" means "mediums" or "necromancers"; "Iye-abarim" means "ruins of the crossing" or "ruins on the other side."

The Israelites move on from these two places with ominous names to the Wadi Zered and from there to the Arnon, which forms the northern boundary of Moab. They arrive at Beer, which means "well," and there the Lord gives them water. Further stations on the journey bring them to the headland of Pisgah that overlooks Jeshimon ("wasteland"). Pisgah is the traditional site for the death of Moses (see Deut 34:1-5). This itinerary is a summary of Israel's whole journey from Mount Hor to the edge of the Promised Land. The entry into the land, however, is a long way off and there are several stories that illustrate the details of the journey summarized here.

Two songs interrupt the itinerary. The first is a song about the river Arnon, the northern border of Moab. Its source is said to be the "Book of the Wars of the LORD." The book is unknown, but the title is an introduction to the stories that will follow. The Lord is about to go to battle in order to give the land to the Israelites just as he swore to their ancestors Abraham, Isaac, and Jacob. The second song is a celebration of the well. The well itself is a

¹⁶From there they went to Beer, which is the well of which the LORD said to Moses, Gather the people together so that I may give them water. ¹⁷Then Israel sang this song:

> Spring up, O well!—so sing to it—
> ¹⁸The well that the princes sank,
>   that the nobles of the people
>   dug,
> With their scepters and their
>   staffs—
>   from the wilderness, a gift.

¹⁹From Beer to Nahaliel, from Nahaliel to Bamoth, ²⁰from Bamoth to the valley in the country of Moab at the headland of Pisgah that overlooks Jeshimon.

Victory over Sihon. ²¹Now Israel sent messengers to Sihon, king of the Amorites, with the message, ²²"Let us pass through your land. We will not turn aside into any field or vineyard, nor will we drink any well water, but we will go straight along the King's Highway until we have passed through your territory." ²³Sihon, however, would not permit Israel to pass through his territory, but mustered all his forces and advanced against Israel into the wilderness. When he reached Jahaz, he engaged Israel in battle. ²⁴But Israel put him to the sword, and took possession of his land from the Arnon to the Jabbok and as far as Jazer of the Ammonites, for Jazer is the boundary of the Ammonites. ²⁵Israel seized all the towns here, and Israel settled in all the towns of the Amorites, in Heshbon and all its dependencies. ²⁶For Heshbon was the city of Sihon, king of the Amorites, who had fought against the former king of Moab and had taken all his land from him as far as the Arnon. ²⁷That is why the poets say:

> "Come to Heshbon, let it be
>   rebuilt,
>   let Sihon's city be firmly
>   constructed.
> ²⁸For fire went forth from Heshbon
>   and a blaze from the city of
>   Sihon;
> It consumed Ar of Moab
>   and swallowed up the high
>   places of the Arnon.
> ²⁹Woe to you, Moab!
>   You are no more, people of
>   Chemosh!

---

sign that the wilderness period is over; the gift of water will be available in the land they are approaching.

21:21-32 Victory over Sihon

The Israelites, having crossed the Arnon, now reach the territory of the Amorites. They make the same request of Sihon that they made to the king of Edom omitting the recital of previous history and reminder of family relationship (see 20:14-16). Edom had refused the request and threatened violence; Sihon not only refuses but engages Israel in battle. The Israelites are victorious and seize the territory of the Amorites. Then they sing a song just as they did after the crossing of the sea. This song, however, does not celebrate Israel's victory. Rather it commemorates Sihon's earlier victory over Moab when the Amorites pushed the Moabites back south of the

He let his sons become fugitives
and his daughters be taken
captive by the Amorite
king Sihon.
³⁰From Heshbon to Dibon their
dominion is no more;
Ar is laid waste; fires blaze as
far as Medeba."

³¹So Israel settled in the land of the Amorites. ³²Moses sent spies to Jazer; and the Israelites captured it with its dependencies and dispossessed the Amorites who were there.

Victory over Og. ³³Then they turned and went up along the road to Bashan. But Og, king of Bashan, advanced against them with all his forces to give battle at Edrei. ³⁴The LORD, however, said to Moses: Do not fear him; for into your hand I deliver him with all his forces and his land. You will do to him as you did to Sihon, king of the Amorites, who reigned in Heshbon. ³⁵So they struck him down with his sons and all his forces, until not a survivor was left to him, and they took possession of his land.

Arnon. Is the recollection of this song a taunt against Sihon who has now lost this same territory? Or is it just a familiar song, remembered because they are now in Heshbon, Sihon's former capital?

21:33–22:1 Victory over Og

As the Israelites press farther north, another king, Og of Bashan, engages them in battle. Israel, however, cannot lose as long as they are faithful to the Lord and acknowledge that they win only by God's power. So Israel takes possession of the whole area on the east side of the Jordan River. The capture of the territory legitimates Israel's later settlement in the area east of the Dead Sea and the Jordan. The tribes of Reuben and Gad will settle in the area of Sihon to the south and half the tribe of Manasseh will settle to the north in Og's former kingdom (see Num 32; Deut 3:12-20; Josh 1:12-16; 12:6).

Sihon, king of the Amorites, and Og, king of Bashan, are well known throughout biblical literature. Deuteronomy repeats the story of their defeat (Deut 2:24–3:11) and adds the detail that Og was one of the giants that the people feared so much (see Num 13:32-33); his bed was almost fourteen feet long (Deut 3:11). Rahab of Jericho and the Gibeonites know the story when Israel enters the land (Josh 2:10; 9:10). After the Babylonian exile Nehemiah praises God for this victory as part of his recital of God's gifts to the people (Neh 9:22). Everyone who prays the Psalms acknowledges this event as a sign of God's great love for the people (Pss 135:11; 136:19-20).

After the victory over Sihon and Og, Israel encamps by the Jordan River across from Jericho. There they will stay until Joshua leads them across to take possession of the land of promise.

22 ¹Then the Israelites moved on and encamped in the plains of Moab on the other side of the Jordan opposite Jericho.

Balaam Summoned. ²Now Balak, son of Zippor, saw all that Israel did to the Amorites, ³and Moab feared the Israelites greatly because they were numerous. Moab was in dread of the Israelites. ⁴So Moab said to the elders of Midian, "Now this horde will devour everything around us as an ox devours the grass of the field." At that time Balak, son of Zippor, was king of Moab; ⁵and he sent messengers to Balaam, son of Beor, at Pethor on the river, in the land of the Ammonites, to summon him with these words, "A people has come out of Egypt! They have covered up the earth and are settling down opposite me! ⁶Now come, curse this people for me, since they are stronger than I am. Perhaps I may be able to defeat them and drive them out of the land. For I know that whoever you bless is blessed and whoever you curse is cursed." ⁷So the elders of Moab and the elders of Midian, themselves experts in divination, left and went to Balaam, to whom they gave Balak's message. ⁸He said to them, "Stay

22:2-14 Balaam summoned

A cycle of stories about the seer Balaam is inserted into the narrative about Israel's advance toward the Promised Land. Balak, king of Moab, is fearful of the power of the Israelites. He has seen how they defeated Sihon and Og; he is aware that this great multitude of people is using up the resources of the surrounding area. So he summons Balaam, son of Beor, to place a curse on Israel. Balak's hope may be that the curse will weaken Israel to the point that he can defeat them and drive them away. When Balak's messengers arrive, however, Balaam tells them he does not act on his own; he must ask God. God forbids him to go because the people he is to curse are already blessed, so Balaam sends a refusal to Balak.

It is unclear from the biblical stories where Balaam's home is. It is sometimes assumed that he is from Syria. In his first oracle (Num 23:7) Balaam says that he has come from Aram (= Syria), from the mountains of Qedem (or the eastern mountains), a mountain range in Syria. Numbers 22:5 states he is from "Pethor on the river"; the "river" is usually a reference to the Euphrates. This same text, however, also says that Pethor is "in the land of the Amaw," which may mean simply "his people." NABRE emends to "Ammonites." Not only is it more likely that Balak would look for a seer close to his own neighborhood, but evidence outside the Bible also supports the conjecture that Balaam is from the Amorite territory east of the Jordan. A seer named Balaam, son of Beor, is known through texts found at Deir ᶜAlla, a site in the Valley of Sukkoth not too far north of where Israel is said to be encamped in Numbers 22:1.

here overnight, and I will give you whatever answer the LORD gives me." So the princes of Moab lodged with Balaam.

⁹Then God came to Balaam and said: Who are these men with you? ¹⁰Balaam answered God, "Balak, son of Zippor, king of Moab, sent me the message: ¹¹'This people that has come out of Egypt has covered up the earth. Now come, lay a curse on them for me; perhaps I may be able to fight them and drive them out.'" ¹²But God said to Balaam: Do not go with them and do not curse this people, for they are blessed. ¹³The next morning Balaam arose and told the princes of Balak, "Go back to your own country, for the LORD has refused to let me go with you." ¹⁴So the princes of Moab went back to Balak with the report, "Balaam refused to come with us."

Second Appeal to Balaam. ¹⁵Balak yet again sent princes, who were more numerous and more distinguished than the others. ¹⁶On coming to Balaam they told him, "Thus says Balak, son of Zippor: Please do not refuse to come to me. ¹⁷I will reward you very handsomely and will do anything you ask of me. Come, lay a curse on this people for me." ¹⁸But Balaam replied to Balak's servants, "Even if Balak gave me his house full of silver and gold, I could not do anything, small or great, contrary to the command of the LORD, my God. ¹⁹But, you too stay here overnight, so that I may learn what else the LORD may say to me." ²⁰That night God came to Balaam and said to him: If these men have come to summon you, go back with them; yet only on the condition that you do exactly as I tell you. ²¹So the next morning when Balaam arose, he saddled his donkey, and went off with the princes of Moab.

The Talking Donkey. ²²But now God's anger flared up at him for going, and the angel of the LORD took up a

---

22:15-21 Second appeal to Balaam

Balak is not so easily deterred; he sends a more impressive delegation to pressure Balaam into coming and promises a handsome reward. Balaam insists he can act only with God's authorization, so again he awaits a night vision. This second time God permits him to go, but warns that he must act totally according to God's design. Throughout this section God is identified through the generic term *ʾelohim* (God; 22:9, 10, 12, 18, 20) and by the proper name of Israel's God *Yahweh* (English, LORD; 22:8, 13, 18, 19). The Israelite author assumes that the only god who could be inspiring Balaam is the Lord. This non-Israelite prophet does God's work just as Israel's prophets do. A prophet is a messenger and must deliver the message exactly as the sender intends. Israel's prophets speak the Lord's word; Balaam too will speak only the message God gives him.

22:22-40 The talking donkey

This section is a fable inserted to illustrate the dependence of the prophet on God. The insertion is marked by two repetitions: First, in 22:21, Balaam

position on the road as his adversary. As Balaam was riding along on his donkey, accompanied by two of his servants, [23]the donkey saw the angel of the Lord standing in the road with sword drawn. The donkey turned off the road and went into the field, and Balaam beat the donkey to bring her back on the road. [24]Then the angel of the Lord stood in a narrow lane between vineyards with a stone wall on each side. [25]When the donkey saw the angel of the Lord there, she pressed against the wall; and since she squeezed Balaam's leg against the wall, he beat her again. [26]Then the angel of the Lord again went ahead, and stood next in a passage so narrow that there was no room to move either to the right or to the left. [27]When the donkey saw the angel of the Lord there, she lay down under Balaam. Balaam's anger flared up and he beat the donkey with his stick.

---

goes off with the princes of Moab and in 22:35 it is again noted that the princes go with him. In between he seems to be accompanied only by two servants and his donkey. Second, in 22:20 God tells Balaam to go with the men but to say only what God tells him; a similar phrase is repeated in 22:35. In between God seems to be angry that Balaam has set off on this journey.

The story makes fun of Balaam. Three times the angel of the Lord stands in his way to stop him; three times the donkey sees the angel but the seer does not. When Balaam beats the donkey a third time, she asks why he is being so cruel. Then the Lord, who opened the donkey's mouth, also opens Balaam's eyes and he sees the angel. The angel (who is really the Lord himself) tells him that he is against this journey. Had Balaam not stopped, the angel would have killed him but spared the donkey. Balaam pleads ignorance and turns to go back home. Here the fable is woven back into the first story: the Lord allows him to go, but only on condition that he delivers God's message.

In the Pentateuch the "angel of the Lord" is often a disguise for the Lord himself as is the case here. Often the angel disappears and the Lord is revealed as the one who is speaking (see Gen 16:7-13; 22:15-16; Exod 3:2-4). The angel also reveals that he is acting as an adversary, who has come to hinder Balaam (22:22, 32). The Hebrew word is *satan*. Throughout the Old Testament period anyone, even God, can be a *satan*; it is only in the New Testament that the developed figure of Satan appears as the personification of evil.

Balak is angry because Balaam has been slow in arriving, but Balaam informs Balak of the truth that has been emphasized throughout this chapter: He can act only when God sends him and speak only when God gives him the words. Balak then offers a sacrifice for the purpose of having meat for a feast to celebrate Balaam's arrival.

²⁸Then the LORD opened the mouth of the donkey, and she asked Balaam, "What have I done to you that you beat me these three times?" ²⁹"You have acted so willfully against me," said Balaam to the donkey, "that if I only had a sword at hand, I would kill you here and now." ³⁰But the donkey said to Balaam, "Am I not your donkey, on which you have always ridden until now? Have I been in the habit of treating you this way before?" "No," he replied.

³¹Then the LORD opened Balaam's eyes, so that he saw the angel of the LORD standing on the road with sword drawn; and he knelt and bowed down to the ground. ³²But the angel of the LORD said to him: "Why have you beaten your donkey these three times? I have come as an adversary because this rash journey of yours is against my will. ³³When the donkey saw me, she turned away from me these three times. If she had not turned away from me, you are the one I would have killed, though I would have spared her." ³⁴Then Balaam said to the angel of the LORD, "I have sinned. Yet I did not know that you took up a position to oppose my journey. Since it has displeased you, I will go back home." ³⁵But the angel of the LORD said to Balaam: "Go with the men; but you may say only what I tell you." So Balaam went on with the princes of Balak.

³⁶When Balak heard that Balaam was coming, he went out to meet him at Ar-Moab on the border formed by the Arnon, at its most distant point. ³⁷And Balak said to Balaam, "Did I not send an urgent summons to you? Why did you not come to me? Did you think I could not reward you?" ³⁸Balaam answered Balak, "Well, I have come to you after all. But what power have I to say anything? I can speak only what God puts in my mouth." ³⁹Then Balaam went with Balak, and they came to Kiriath-huzoth. ⁴⁰Here Balak sacrificed oxen and sheep, and sent portions to Balaam and to the princes who were with him.

The First Oracle. ⁴¹The next morning Balak took Balaam up on Bamoth-baal,

22:41–23:12 The first oracle

Early the next morning Balak and Balaam prepare for Balaam's task. Tension rises from the different motives of the two men: Balak is intending that Balaam will curse Israel and thus weaken it (22:6, 11, 17); Balaam has been insisting that he can speak only what God puts in his mouth (22:38, see 22:13, 18-19). Balak chooses the spot for the event, a place where Balaam can see "some of the people" whom he is to curse. Balaam gives instructions for inviting God to be present: Balak is to build seven altars and offer a bull and a ram on each. This is a significant sacrifice. Bulls and rams were valuable animals; the number seven signifies completeness. Surely God will respond.

Balaam goes out to meet the Lord. This non-Israelite seer cannot assume that Israel's God will speak to him even though he knows God's proper

and from there he could see some of the people.

23 ¹Then Balaam said to Balak, "Build me seven altars here, and here prepare seven bulls and seven rams for me." ²So Balak did as Balaam had ordered, and Balak and Balaam offered a bull and a ram on each altar. ³Balaam said to Balak, "Stand here by your burnt offering while I go over there. Perhaps the LORD will meet me, and then I will tell you whatever he lets me see." And so he went out on the barren height. ⁴Then God met Balaam, and Balak said to him: "I have erected the seven altars, and have offered a bull and a ram on each altar." ⁵The LORD put an utterance in Balaam's mouth, and said: Go back to Balak, and speak accordingly. ⁶So he went back to Balak, who was still standing by his burnt offering together with all the princes of Moab. ⁷Then Balaam recited his poem:

---

name, Yahweh (22:8, 13, 18, 19; 23:3), and claims him as his own God (22:18). Thus he walks around seeking an omen indicating what he should do. God, however, has a relationship with this man and not only comes to meet him but puts a word in his mouth just as he does with the other prophets (see Jer 1:9).

Balaam returns to Balak and recites his *mashal*. The *mashal* is a wisdom saying, either short (a proverb) or long (a parable). Usually the *mashal* has a "sting in its tail," a message that the hearer may not want but really needs. The use of the word *mashal* suggests that Balaam is a wise man, a sage, since the *mashal* is usually not associated with prophets. (Ezekiel, however, does tell several parables and contradicts several proverbs [Ezek 12:22-23; 17:2; 18:2-3; 24:3] and is even called a "spinner of parables" [Ezek 21:5].) Philo, a first-century Jewish writer, calls Balaam a *magus*, that is, "wise man" (compare the *magi* in Matt 2).

Balak's first *mashal* begins with his impossible task: he was summoned to curse Israel, but where can he find power to curse one whom God has not cursed? Thus, instead of cursing (or blessing), he expresses his awe at the greatness of this people spread out below him. This people lives independently without need of allies among the nations. Their multitude, which frightened Balak just as it worried Pharaoh (Exod 1:9), is beyond counting. God's promise to Abraham that his descendants would be like the sand on the seashore (Gen 22:17) has been fulfilled: they are like the dust that their travels have stirred up in the desert. Balaam is so overcome at the sight of this people that he prays to be like them.

Balak is enraged and claims that Balaam has even blessed the people although he has not. Balaam's defense is simple: He can say only what the Lord puts in his mouth. He is a faithful prophet.

From Aram Balak has led me here,
   Moab's king, from the moun-
      tains of Qedem:
"Come, curse for me Jacob,
   come, denounce Israel."
[8]How can I lay a curse on the one
   whom God has not cursed?
How denounce the one whom
     the Lord has not de-
     nounced?
[9]For from the top of the crags I see
   him,
   from the heights I behold him.
Here is a people that lives apart
   and does not reckon itself
      among the nations.
[10]Who has ever counted the dust of
   Jacob,
   who numbered Israel's dust-
     cloud?
May I die the death of the just,
   may my end be like theirs!

[11]"What have you done to me?" cried Balak to Balaam. "It was to lay a curse on my foes that I brought you here; but instead, you have blessed them!" [12]Balaam replied, "Is it not what the Lord puts in my mouth that I take care to repeat?"

The Second Oracle. [13]Then Balak said to him, "Please come with me to another place from which you can see them; but you will see only some, not all of them, and from there lay a curse on them for me." [14]So he brought him to a lookout post on the top of Pisgah, where he built seven altars and offered a bull and a ram on each of them. [15]Balaam then said to Balak, "Stand here by your burnt offering, while I seek a meeting over there." [16]Then the Lord met Balaam, and, having put an utterance in his mouth, said to him: Return to Balak, and speak ac-

23:13-26 The second oracle

Balak decides to try another place; perhaps at the previous site Balaam could see too many of these people. The same sacrifices are offered; Balaam again goes out to seek the Lord, who meets him and puts a new word in his mouth. When Balaam returns to Balak, the king asks, "What did the Lord say?" Balak has at least learned the source of Balaam's oracles even if he does not like them.

Balaam's second *mashal* is addressed to Balak. It is a lesson regarding who the Lord is. This is not a weak human being who can be manipulated; rather, this is the faithful God who has power to bring his word to fulfillment. Balaam was summoned to bless and he must bless. What is more, this people whom Balak fears is stronger than he imagined. The Lord, who brought them out of Egypt, remains with them and gives them terrible strength. Balak has miscalculated: these people are not an ox eating up the grass of the field (22:4); they are a lion ready to attack and devour their prey. Balak cannot defeat them.

Balak now tries to minimize the damage. He orders Balaam neither to curse nor to bless these people. Balaam, however, cannot even agree to this: Whatever the Lord says, he must announce.

cordingly. ¹⁷So he went to Balak, who was still standing by his burnt offering together with the princes of Moab. When Balak asked him, "What did the LORD say?" ¹⁸Balaam recited his poem:

> Rise, Balak, and listen;
>> give ear to my testimony, son of Zippor!
> ¹⁹God is not a human being who speaks falsely,
>> nor a mortal, who feels regret.
> Is God one to speak and not act,
>> to decree and not bring it to pass?
> ²⁰I was summoned to bless;
>> I will bless; I cannot revoke it!
> ²¹Misfortune I do not see in Jacob,
>> nor do I see misery in Israel.
> The LORD, their God, is with them;
>> among them is the war-cry of their King.
> ²²They have the like of a wild ox's horns:
>> God who brought them out of Egypt.

> ²³No, there is no augury against Jacob,
>> nor divination against Israel.
> Now it is said of Jacob,
>> of Israel, "Look what God has done!"
> ²⁴Here is a people that rises up like a lioness,
>> and gets up like a lion;
> It does not rest till it has devoured its prey
>> and has drunk the blood of the slain.

²⁵"Neither lay a curse on them nor bless them," said Balak to Balaam. ²⁶But Balaam answered Balak, "Did I not tell you, 'Everything the LORD tells me I must do'?"

The Third Oracle. ²⁷Then Balak said to Balaam, "Come, let me bring you to another place; perhaps God will approve of your laying a curse on them for me from there." ²⁸So he took Balaam to the top of Peor, that overlooks

23:27–24:13 The third oracle

Balak stations Balaam at yet a third place. This time he is not concerned about what Balaam can see (23:13) but about whether God will approve a curse from here. Gradually Balak is learning who is in charge. The same sacrifices are again offered.

Balaam, however, has changed his method. He recognizes that God will be pleased not with a curse but with a blessing for Israel. He does not need to walk around to seek omens; he is filled with the spirit of God. This puts him in good company: The spirit of God (or the Lord) inspires leaders (Othniel, Judg 3:10; Gideon, Judg 6:34; Jephthah, Judg 11:29; Samson, Judg 13:25; 14:6, 19; 15:14; Saul, 1 Sam 10:6, 10; 11:6; 19:23; David, 1 Sam 16:13; 2 Sam 23:2; the ideal king, Isa 11:2), wise persons (Joseph, Gen 41:38; Bezalel, Exod 31:3; 35:31), and prophets (Elijah, 1 Kgs 18:12; Ezekiel, Ezek 11:5, 24; 37:1; Micah, Mic 3:8).

Thus inspired, Balaam recites his *mashal*. He begins with a solemn introduction: This poem and the next one are identified by the technical term

Jeshimon. ²⁹Balaam then said to Balak, "Build me seven altars here; and here prepare for me seven bulls and seven rams." ³⁰And Balak did as Balaam had ordered, offering a bull and a ram on each altar.

24 ¹Balaam, however, perceiving that the LORD was pleased to bless Israel, did not go aside as before to seek omens, but turned his gaze toward the wilderness. ²When Balaam looked up and saw Israel encamped, tribe by tribe, the spirit of God came upon him, ³and he recited his poem:

> The oracle of Balaam, son of Beor,
>> the oracle of the man whose eye is true,
> ⁴The oracle of one who hears what God says,
>> and knows what the Most High knows,
> Of one who sees what the Almighty sees,
>> in rapture and with eyes unveiled:

"oracle" (Hebrew *neʾum*; 24:3-4, 15-16). This term is commonly used by prophets (356 times) to identify a message from the Lord (e.g., Isa 41:14; Jer 1:8; Ezek 37:14; Hos 11:11; Joel 2:12; Amos 2:11; Mic 4:6; Nah 2:14; Zeph 1:2-3; Hag 1:13; Zech 1:3-4; Mal 1:3). Not only Balaam's vocabulary, but also his claim to authority puts him squarely in the prophetic tradition. He describes himself as one who sees as God sees, hears what God says, and knows what God knows. The message he delivers will be the message of God; he has received it in a prophetic trance but with his eyes open.

He identifies God with three names that were originally the names of Canaanite gods but that have become descriptions of Yahweh, the God of Israel: El, the head of the Canaanite pantheon; Shaddai (translated "Almighty"; see Gen 17:1; 28:3; 35:11; Exod 6:3), god of the mountains; and Elyon ("Most High"), the god whom Melchizedek serves (Gen 14:18-22).

This oracle is addressed to the people, Israel ("you/your" in 24:5, 9). It is a hymn of praise, echoed in the psalms: "How lovely your dwelling, / O LORD of hosts" (Ps 84:2); "How good it is, how pleasant, / where the people dwell as one!" (Ps 133:1). Israel itself is a testimony to God's fidelity: God's promise of fertility has been fulfilled (see Gen 17:5-6); the prophet sees this people like well-watered trees. The promise of land (see Gen 12:7) is also about to be fulfilled, but it will require struggle. The people will crush all their enemies as a lion devours prey. The refrain from the second oracle recurs (see 23:22), along with a reference to a later victory. As an example of Israel's power, the final editor anticipates King Saul's tenth-century defeat of the Amalekites under their king, Agag (1 Sam 15:1-8). Balaam ends his oracle with a beatitude and a curse, repeating the promise to Abraham: "I will bless those who bless you and curse those who curse you" (Gen 12:3).

⁵How pleasant are your tents, Jacob;
   your encampments, Israel!
⁶Like palm trees spread out,
   like gardens beside a river,
Like aloes the LORD planted,
   like cedars beside water;
⁷Water will drip from their buckets,
   their seed will have plentiful
   water;
Their king will rise higher than Agag
   and their dominion will be ex-
   alted.
⁸They have the like of a wild ox's
   horns:
God who brought them out of
   Egypt.
They will devour hostile nations,
   break their bones, and crush
   their loins.
⁹Crouching, they lie like a lion,
   or like a lioness; who will arouse
   them?

Blessed are those who bless you,
   and cursed are those who curse
      you!

¹⁰In a blaze of anger at Balaam, Balak clapped his hands and said to him, "It was to lay a curse on my foes that I summoned you here; yet three times now you have actually blessed them! ¹¹Now flee to your home. I promised to reward you richly, but the LORD has withheld the reward from you!" ¹²Balaam replied to Balak, "Did I not even tell the messengers whom you sent to me, ¹³'Even if Balak gave me his house full of silver and gold, I could not of my own accord do anything, good or evil, contrary to the command of the LORD'? Whatever the LORD says I must say.

The Fourth Oracle. ¹⁴"But now that I am about to go to my own people, let

---

Balaam's blessings and curses are not according to Balak's wishes, however. In his fury the king dismisses Balaam and refuses to pay him. But Balaam had never agreed to the payment (22:18); instead he has consistently told Balak that he can proclaim only what the Lord gives him. He can bless and curse only those whom God blesses and curses.

24:14-25 The fourth oracle

Balak may be finished with Balaam, but the prophet is not finished with the king. He has a warning for Balak regarding Israel. This last oracle begins with the same claim to authority as the previous one. Balaam warns Balak, king of Moab, that a future ruler of Israel will crush Moab along with the rest of Transjordan. The future ruler is imaged as a star and a scepter. In the tenth century David did defeat Moab and made it a vassal state; Moab remained under Israelite control until the revolt of the Moabite king Mesha (see 2 Kgs 3:4-5). In the ensuing centuries as further difficulties arose, the people began to look for a new David, an anointed king (=messiah) who would shepherd them with his scepter/staff as David did (see Mic 5:1-4; 7:14).

Early Christian writers understood Balaam's words in terms of Christ and connected his vision of a star to the story of the magi in Matthew 2.

me warn you what this people will do to your people in the days to come." [15]Then he recited his poem:

The oracle of Balaam, son of Beor,
  the oracle of the man whose eye
    is true,
[16]The oracle of one who hears what
    God says,
  and knows what the Most High
    knows,
Of one who sees what the Almighty
    sees,
  in rapture and with eyes
    unveiled.
  [17]I see him, though not now;
  I observe him, though not near:
A star shall advance from Jacob,
  and a scepter shall rise from
    Israel,

That will crush the brows of
    Moab,
  and the skull of all the Sethites,
[18]Edom will be dispossessed,
  and no survivor is left in Seir.
Israel will act boldly,
  [19]and Jacob will rule his foes.

[20]Upon seeing Amalek, Balaam recited his poem:

First of the nations is Amalek,
  but their end is to perish forever.

[21]Upon seeing the Kenites, he recited his poem:

Though your dwelling is safe,
  and your nest is set on a cliff;
[22]Yet Kain will be destroyed
  when Asshur takes you captive.

Jewish interpreters also regarded this passage as an expression of messianic hope. The messianic aspirations that circled around Simon ben Kosiba who led a revolt against Rome (132–135 A.D.) are indicated by his nickname, Bar Kokhba, "son of the star."

Balaam continues his oracle by describing the fate of the Sethites, Edomites, Amalekites, Kenites, and Ishmaelites. Edom is just south of Moab, south of the Dead Sea. Although their name (another name for Esau) indicates a family tie with Israel (=Jacob), they are traditional enemies. David conquered Edom but they regained independence during the reign of Solomon. They were among those who plundered what was left of Judah after Nebuchadnezzar's invasion in 587 B.C. The Amalekites are described as "first of the nations," either because they were the first to engage Israel in battle (Exod 17:8-16) or because they were an ancient Canaanite people. Although they were "first," their "end" is to perish before Israel. They were finally subdued by David (1 Sam 30:1-18). The Kenites are usually regarded as friendly to Israel (see 1 Sam 15:6; 27:10). Perhaps the oracle against them reflects the traditional belief that they were descended from Cain and a distrust of their profession as metalworkers (Gen 4:22).

The other two groups are more difficult to identify. Sethites, descendants of Seth, Adam's son, may be a generic term for human beings (see Gen 4:25) or they may be a people otherwise called the Shutu, who are mentioned in

²³Upon seeing [the Ishmaelites?] he recited his poem:

Alas, who shall survive of Ishmael,
²⁴to deliver them from the hands
of the Kittim?
When they have conquered Asshur
and conquered Eber,
They too shall perish forever.

²⁵Then Balaam set out on his journey home; and Balak also went his way.

25 Worship of Baal of Peor. ¹While Israel was living at Shittim, the people profaned themselves by prostituting themselves with the Moabite women. ²These then invited the people to the sacrifices of their god, and the

the Amarna letters of the fourteenth century B.C. The final group named in the oracle (Hebrew *sumo ʾel*) is unknown. The Septuagint interprets this word to connote Og (see Num 21:33-35). The NABRE translators have interpreted it to mean the Ishmaelites, descendants of Abraham's son, who live in the southern desert. Whoever these people are, Balaam announces that they will be attacked by the Kittim, people of Cyprus, after they have conquered Assyria and the otherwise unknown Eber. The point of the oracle is that Israel's enemies, including Moab, will not survive.

After these chapters in which Balaam claims the Lord as his God and faithfully proclaims his word, his reputation suffers. Only the prophet Micah recalls his steadfastness in resisting Balak's plans (Mic 6:5). He is blamed for Israel's infidelity at Baal Peor (Num 31:15-16; see Josh 13:22) and, in contrast to the story here, is portrayed as actually proclaiming a curse against Israel, which God turned into a blessing (Deut 23:6; Josh 24:9-10; Neh 13:2). He fares even worse in the New Testament where he is not only made responsible for the Baal Peor incident (Rev 2:14) but is also described, in direct contradiction of this story, as greedy for gain (2 Pet 2:15; Jude 11).

25:1-5 Worship of Baal of Peor

Careful reading is necessary to understand this chapter. Two stories have been woven together, producing several ambiguities. The first story involves Moabite women; the second centers on a Midianite woman. The first story concludes with the execution of the guilty parties as does the second, but at some indeterminate point a plague also breaks out. In later literature both stories have been interpreted in sexual terms, but nowhere in the chapter is there an explicit description of sexual activity.

The first story represents the earlier, pre-Priestly tradition. It is introduced with the announcement: "[T]he people profaned themselves by prostituting themselves with the Moabite women." Two verbs describe their action: "profaned" and "prostituting themselves." The verb translated

people ate of the sacrifices and bowed down to their god. ³Israel thereby attached itself to the Baal of Peor, and the LORD's anger flared up against Israel. ⁴The LORD said to Moses: Gather all the leaders of the people, and publicly execute them before the LORD, that the blazing wrath of the LORD may turn away from Israel. ⁵So Moses told the Israelite judges, "Each of you kill those of his men who have attached themselves to the Baal of Peor."

"profaned" (Hebrew *hillel*) is used in many contexts, most having to do with breaking God's law. For example, one profanes oneself by working on the sabbath (Exod 31:14), by sacrificing children to Molech (Lev 18:21), by swearing falsely (Lev 19:12), or by not keeping a vow (Num 30:3). The verb translated "prostituting themselves" seems to suggest a sexual context. However, it is a common idiom also for worshiping other gods. The covenant relationship with God is compared to a marriage relationship, most notably by Hosea (chs. 1–3; cf. Jer 3:1). So worshiping another god is imaged as adultery against the people's "husband," Yahweh (e.g., Lev 20:5-6; Deut 31:16; Judg 2:17; 1 Chr 5:25). This is the context for the story in Numbers 25:1-5.

The Moabite women invite the people—presumably both men and women—to share in the sacrifices to their god, the Baal of Peor. In one sense, this is as simple as inviting them to dinner. In most of the ancient Near East during this period, meat was not eaten unless the animal had first been offered to a god in sacrifice. (The same problem, whether to eat the meat set before one in someone else's house, faced Christians in Paul's time; see 1 Cor 8.) The Israelites attended the sacrifice, ate the meal, and thus honored the god.

The meal itself is the central element of the sacrifice and the greatest problem. To eat together, to share the same food, is to share the same life. For this reason, a meal is one way of sealing a covenant (see Gen 31:45-54; Exod 24:11). This principle is evident also in Israel's sacrificial tradition: in sacrifices other than the whole burnt offering, part of the sacrifice is offered to God (by burning) and part is consumed by the worshipers (e.g., Lev 7:11-21). Thus by eating the sacrifice "with" the Baal of Peor, the Israelites have attached themselves to another god and been unfaithful to the Lord. The people's sin is idolatry.

In anger the Lord commands Moses to execute all the leaders of the people by impaling them in the sun (i.e., "publicly"). The leaders are apparently considered responsible for the wrongdoing of the people. The punishment is unusual in the Old Testament, occurring only one other

Zeal of Phinehas. ⁶At this a certain Israelite came and brought in a Midianite woman to his kindred in the view of Moses and of the whole Israelite community, while they were weeping at the entrance of the tent of meeting. ⁷When Phinehas, son of Eleazar, son of Aaron the priest, saw this, he rose up from the assembly, and taking a spear in his hand, ⁸followed the Israelite into the tent where he pierced the two of them, the Israelite and the woman. Thus the plague upon the Israelites was checked; ⁹but the dead from the plague were twenty-four thousand.

¹⁰Then the LORD said to Moses: ¹¹Phinehas, son of Eleazar, son of Aaron the priest, has turned my anger from the Israelites by his being as jealous among them as I am; that is why I did not put

---

time (2 Sam 21:5-9). Not only is the execution public, but burial is probably denied the victims (see Deut 21:23). Moses modifies the Lord's command, however, by instructing the judges to kill only those who are guilty.

25:6-15 Zeal of Phinehas

The second story is from the Priestly tradition. As it begins the community is weeping at the entrance to the tent of meeting, presumably in mourning for those who have been killed. An Israelite man brings a Midianite woman in before the whole community. Immediately Phinehas assassinates both of them. Then the plague is stopped.

There are more questions than answers in this story. No reason is given for the woman's presence and no description is given of what the man and woman do. No reason is given for the action of Phinehas, but the consequence is the cooling of God's anger and the cessation of the plague. The plague also comes as a surprise. When did it begin and why? The only information provided is that twenty-four thousand people have been killed.

Interpreters have assumed that the Israelite man, later identified as Zimri, married the Midianite woman. There is a great fear that marriage to non-Israelite women will lead men into worshiping other gods (Exod 34:15-16). Even Solomon is said to have been led astray by his foreign wives (1 Kgs 11:1-8). Interpreters also assume that Zimri and Cozbi were having sexual intercourse when Phinehas killed them. Neither assumption is explicitly supported by the text, however. Phinehas follows them to "the tent" (Hebrew *qubbah*). This Hebrew word occurs only here in the Old Testament and signifies something like a canopy or alcove. It is not clear whether this is part of the tent of meeting or a separate enclosure. Perhaps it is related to the tent shrines of nomadic Arabs called *qubbah* in Arabic. In that case, Zimri may have brought Cozbi in to perform a cultic ministry, pleading with God to end the plague just as Balak brought Balaam in to curse Israel.

an end to the Israelites in my jealousy. ¹²Announce, therefore, that I hereby give him my covenant of peace, ¹³which shall be for him and for his descendants after him the covenant of an everlasting priesthood, because he was jealous on behalf of his God and thus made expiation for the Israelites.

¹⁴The name of the slain Israelite, the one slain with the Midianite woman, was Zimri, son of Salu, prince of a Simeonite ancestral house. ¹⁵The name of the slain Midianite woman was Cozbi, daughter of Zur, who was head of a clan, an ancestral house, in Midian.

Whether it is intermarriage with a foreigner or a cultic ritual performed by a foreigner, however, the action is understood by Phinehas as an affront to the Lord. The wrongdoing in this story is the same as that in the first story: the movement toward worship of other gods.

Phinehas is praised for his rapid response to the threatening situation: "Then Phinehas rose to intervene, / and the plague was brought to a halt. / This was counted for him as a righteous deed / for all generations to come" (Ps 106:30-31). He is promised a covenant of peace and a covenant of everlasting priesthood. The covenant of peace suggests that, first of all, he will be protected from vengeance by the family of Zimri. It also indicates that he will remain in God's favor and friendship. In the book of Malachi God states that the covenant with Levi is just such a covenant: "My covenant with him was the life and peace which I gave him, / and the fear he had for me, / standing in awe of my name" (Mal 2:5). Through this action Phinehas is also established as the one through whom the priestly line continues. He is the only son of Aaron's son Eleazar according to the genealogy in Exodus (Exod 6:25; see Num 20:26-28). After the people are settled in the Promised Land he ministers to the ark of the covenant in the shrine at Bethel (Judg 20:28).

Phinehas is said to have been as jealous among the Israelites as the Lord is. The words "jealousy" and "to be jealous" occur twice each in 25:11-13. The Lord is often said to be jealous for the chosen people (e.g., Isa 9:6; 26:11; 42:13; 59:17; Joel 2:18) or for Jerusalem (e.g., Zech 1:14; 8:2). God is even named "the Jealous One": "You shall not bow down to any other god, for the LORD—'Jealous' his name—is a jealous God" (Exod 34:14; cf. Deut 4:24; 5:9; Josh 24:19). English speakers must remember that the words "jealous" and "zealous" have the same root even though their current meanings have separated into negative and positive connotations. To speak of God's "jealousy" or "zeal" is to say that God is passionate about these people and cares deeply. Phinehas has mirrored that passionate zeal.

Vengeance on the Midianites. [16]The Lord then said to Moses: [17]Treat the Midianites as enemies and strike them, [18]for they have been your enemies by the deceitful dealings they had with you regarding Peor and their kinswoman Cozbi, the daughter of a Midianite prince, who was slain at the time of the plague because of Peor.

III. Second Census of a New Generation and Preparation to Enter the Promised Land

26 **The Second Census.** [19]After the plague [1]the Lord said to Moses and Eleazar, son of Aaron the priest: [2]Take a census, by ancestral houses, throughout the community of the Israelites of all those of twenty years or more

---

25:16-18 Vengeance on the Midianites

The incident with the Midianite woman leads to a command to crush the whole people. The Midianites were somehow involved with Balak in arranging with Balaam to curse Israel (see Num 22:4, 7). Cozbi, the catalyst for the previous event, was the daughter of a Midianite prince. The battle against the Midianites will be described in Numbers 31.

Women from the two groups of people who are held responsible in this chapter for Israel's apostasy, the Moabites and the Midianites, have also been a great blessing to Israel. Zipporah, daughter of the priest of Midian, saved the life of Moses, her husband (Exod 4:24-26). Ruth, the Moabite, is an ancestor of David, the king (Ruth 4:13-17).

SECOND CENSUS OF A NEW GENERATION, PREPARATION TO ENTER THE PROMISED LAND
Numbers 26:1–36:13

25:19–26:51 The second census

The primary tradition represented from this point to the end of Numbers is the Priestly tradition. A major interest in this tradition is genealogies, so it is no surprise that another census begins this last section. This is a new generation, however. Apparently the last of the generation that came out of Egypt has died in the plague at Shittim, as God said they would (14:21-23, 28-33). (The pre-Priestly tradition suggests that the old generation has died at the end of Num 20.) Only Caleb, Joshua, and Moses remain from that generation (see 26:64-65). The "little ones" who were under twenty when the spies scouted out the land are now to be counted. The first purpose of the census is to assess military strength (v. 2). Are there enough fighting men to prevail in the struggle for the Promised Land? A second purpose

who are eligible for military service in Israel. [3]So on the plains of Moab along the Jordan at Jericho, Moses and Eleazar the priest enrolled them, [4]those of twenty years or more, as the LORD had commanded Moses.

The Israelites who came out of the land of Egypt were as follows:

[5]Reuben, the firstborn of Israel. The descendants of Reuben by their clans were: through Hanoch, the clan of the Hanochites; through Pallu, the clan of the Palluites; [6]through Hezron, the clan of the Hezronites; through Carmi, the clan of the Carmites. [7]These were the clans of the Reubenites, and those enrolled numbered forty-three thousand seven hundred and thirty.

[8]From Pallu descended Eliab. [9]The sons of Eliab were Nemuel, Dathan, and Abiram—the same Dathan and Abiram, ones designated by the community, who contended with Moses and Aaron as part of Korah's faction when they contended with the LORD. [10]The earth opened its mouth and swallowed them, along with Korah, as a warning. The faction was destroyed when the fire consumed two hundred and fifty men. [11]The descendants of Korah, however, did not die out.

[12]The descendants of Simeon by clans were: through Nemuel, the clan of the Nemuelites; through Jamin, the clan of the Jaminites; through Jachin, the clan of the Jachinites; [13]through Zerah, the clan of the Zerahites; through Shaul, the clan of the Shaulites. [14]These were the clans of the Simeonites, twenty-two thousand two hundred.

[15]The descendants of Gad by clans were: through Zephon, the clan of the

---

has to do with the allotment of the land (see 26:52-56). How much land can each tribe settle and does each tribe need?

This second census parallels the first (see Num 1). The Lord's command to Moses is similar and the order of the tribes is the same with one exception: Manasseh is placed before Ephraim (see Figure 3, p. 14). There are other differences: There is no indication of the date except the notice that the plague has ended (25:19). Eleazar has replaced Aaron who has died. No tribal leaders are designated to assist them. Several generations of each tribe are listed and stories are attached to several individuals.

The significant material in this census is found in the stories, all of which have to do with inheritance. From the tribe of Reuben, Dathan and Abiram from the third generation of descendants are singled out (26:9). They were killed for rebelling against Moses and so their line is removed from the tribal inheritance (see ch. 16). Korah, from the tribe of Levi, is also mentioned here, since the story of his rebellion is told in chapter 16. The narrator is careful to note that, even though Korah died, some of his descendants survived (26:10-11). Several psalms are later attributed to the "sons of Korah" (Pss 42; 44–49; 84–85; 87–88).

Zephonites; through Haggi, the clan of the Haggites; through Shuni, the clan of the Shunites; [16]through Ozni, the clan of the Oznites; through Eri, the clan of the Erites; [17]through Arod, the clan of the Arodites; through Areli, the clan of the Arelites. [18]These were the clans of the descendants of Gad, of whom there were enrolled forty thousand five hundred.

[19]The sons of Judah were Er and Onan. Er and Onan died in the land of Canaan. [20]The descendants of Judah by their clans were: through Shelah, the clan of the Shelahites; through Perez, the clan of the Perezites; through Zerah, the clan of the Zerahites. [21]The descendants of Perez were: through Hezron, the clan of the Hezronites; through Hamul, the clan of the Hamulites. [22]These were the clans of Judah, of whom there were enrolled seventy-six thousand five hundred.

[23]The descendants of Issachar by their clans were: through Tola, the clan of the Tolaites; through Puvah, the clan of the Puvahites; [24]through Jashub, the clan of the Jashubites; through Shimron, the clan of the Shimronites. [25]These were the clans of Issachar, of whom there were enrolled sixty-four thousand three hundred.

[26]The descendants of Zebulun by their clans were: through Sered, the clan of the Seredites; through Elon, the clan of the Elonites; through Jahleel, the clan of the Jahleelites. [27]These were the clans of the Zebulunites, of whom there were enrolled sixty thousand five hundred.

[28]The sons of Joseph were Manasseh and Ephraim. [29]The descendants of Manasseh by clans were: through Machir, the clan of the Machirites. Now Machir begot Gilead: through Gilead, the clan of

The story of Judah's three sons by his first wife is the next to appear (26:19; see Gen 38). Judah arranged for Er to marry Tamar and, when he died, to marry Onan according to the levirate custom. Onan refused to father a son with Tamar, however, and he also died. Judah did not want to lose his third son, so he made Tamar wait. After a long period of time she tricked Judah into having intercourse with her. Tamar's twin sons, Perez and Zerah, appear in this genealogy, replacing the two lost sons of Judah. The line of Perez is taken to the next generation, presumably because he is the ancestor of David. The inheritance will continue through him.

Manasseh is listed before Ephraim, thus holding the significant seventh place in the genealogy (compare Figure 3, p. 14). One reason for this distinction is the story of the daughters of Zelophehad, who occupy the seventh place in the genealogy of Joseph (Joseph, Manasseh, Machir, Gilead, Hepher, Zelophehad, his five daughters). They will initiate a change in the law of inheritance, which previously had applied only to sons. Their full story is told in the next chapter and in chapter 36. The tribe of Manasseh has also increased more since the first census than any other tribe: from 32,200 to 52,700. They will be one of the dominant tribes throughout Israel's history.

the Gileadites. [30]The descendants of Gilead were: through Iezer, the clan of the Iezrites; through Helek, the clan of the Helekites; [31]through Asriel, the clan of the Asrielites; through Shechem, the clan of the Shechemites; [32]through Shemida, the clan of the Shemidaites; through Hepher, the clan of the Hepherites. [33]As for Zelophehad, son of Hepher —he had no sons, but only daughters. The names of the daughters of Zelophehad were Mahlah, Noah, Hoglah, Milcah and Tirzah. [34]These were the clans of Manasseh, and those enrolled numbered fifty-two thousand seven hundred.

[35]These were the descendants of Ephraim by their clans: through Shuthelah, the clan of the Shuthelahites; through Becher, the clan of the Becherites; through Tahan, the clan of the Tahanites. [36]These were the descendants of Shuthelah: through Eran, the clan of the Eranites. [37]These were the clans of the Ephraimites, of whom there were enrolled thirty-two thousand five hundred.

These were the descendants of Joseph by their clans.

[38]The descendants of Benjamin by their clans were: through Bela, the clan of the Belaites; through Ashbel, the clan of the Ashbelites; through Ahiram, the clan of the Ahiramites; [39]through Shupham, the clan of the Shuphamites; through Hupham, the clan of the Huphamites. [40]The sons of Bela were Ard and Naaman: through Ard, the clan of the Ardites; through Naaman, the clan of the Naamites. [41]These were the descendants of Benjamin by their clans, of whom there were enrolled forty-five thousand six hundred.

[42]These were the descendants of Dan by their clans: through Shuham the clan

In the tribe of Asher a daughter, Serah, is named (26:46). Besides the daughters of Zelophehad, she is the only woman named in this genealogy. There are no stories about her, but she is also listed in other genealogies (Gen 46:17; 1 Chr 7:30). The situation of the daughters of Zelophehad does not apply to her since she has brothers and the inheritance continues through them.

Figure 6: Comparison of the Population in the First and Second Censuses

Tribe	Numbers 1	Numbers 26	Tribe	Numbers 1	Numbers 26
Reuben	46,500	43,730	Manasseh	32,200	52,700
Simeon	59,300	22,200	Ephraim	40,500	32,500
Gad	45,650	40,500	Benjamin	35,400	45,600
Judah	74,600	76,500	Dan	62,700	64,400
Issachar	54,400	64,300	Asher	41,500	53,400
Zebulun	57,400	60,500	Naphtali	53,400	45,400

of the Shuhamites. These were the clans of Dan, ⁴³of whom there were enrolled sixty-four thousand four hundred.

⁴⁴The descendants of Asher by their clans were: through Imnah, the clan of the Imnites; through Ishvi, the clan of the Ishvites; through Beriah, the clan of the Beriites; ⁴⁵through Heber, the clan of the Heberites; through Malchiel, the clan of the Malchielites. ⁴⁶The name of Asher's daughter was Serah. ⁴⁷These were the clans of the descendants of Asher, of whom there were enrolled fifty-three thousand four hundred.

⁴⁸The descendants of Naphtali by their clans were: through Jahzeel, the clan of the Jahzeelites; through Guni, the clan of the Gunites; ⁴⁹through Jezer, the clan of the Jezerites; through Shillem, the clan of the Shillemites. ⁵⁰These were the clans of Naphtali, of whom there were enrolled forty-five thousand four hundred.

⁵¹These were the Israelites who were enrolled: six hundred and one thousand seven hundred and thirty.

Allotment of the Land. ⁵²The LORD said to Moses: ⁵³Among these the land shall be divided as their heritage in keeping with the number of people named. ⁵⁴To a large tribe you shall assign a large heritage, to a small tribe a small heritage, each receiving its heritage in proportion to the number enrolled in it. ⁵⁵But the land shall be divided by lot, all inheriting according to the lists of their ancestral tribes. ⁵⁶As the lot falls the heritage of each tribe, large or small, will be assigned.

Census of the Levites. ⁵⁷These were the Levites enrolled by clans: through Gershon, the clan of the Gershonites; through Kohath, the clan of the Kohathites; through Merari, the clan of the Merarites. ⁵⁸These were clans of Levi: the

---

26:52-56 Allotment of the land

The second purpose of the census, the allotment of the land, appears next. Two apparently contradictory methods of distribution are described. The first (vv. 53-54) relates directly to the census: tribes with more people get more land. The second (v. 55) calls for distribution of land by casting lots. This lottery method seems to ignore the relative size of each tribe. Verse 56 is an attempt to combine the two methods, which seems to be what Joshua did for each tribe, with the exception of the tribes that remained in Transjordan: Reuben, Gad, and the half-tribe of Manasseh (see Josh 13–20).

26:57-65 Census of the Levites

The Levites are again omitted from the regular census (see 1:47-53). They are not to inherit the land along with the other tribes (Num 18:20-24; 26:62; Deut 10:8-9; compare Josh 21). The genealogy of Levi begins as usual with Gershon, Kohath, and Merari (see Gen 46:11; Exod 6:16; Num 3:17). The next verse (26:58), however, interrupts the list with clans that, in other genealogies, belong to the next generations: Libni, son of Gershon (Exod 6:17; Num 3:18, 21); Hebron, son of Kohath (Exod 6:18; Num 3:19, 27); Mahli

clan of the Libnites, the clan of the He-bronites, the clan of the Mahlites, the clan of the Mushites, the clan of the Ko-rahites.

Now Kohath begot Amram, ⁵⁹whose wife was named Jochebed. She was the daughter of Levi, born to Levi in Egypt. To Amram she bore Aaron and Moses and Miriam their sister. ⁶⁰To Aaron were born Nadab and Abihu, Eleazar and Ithamar. ⁶¹But Nadab and Abihu died when they offered unauthorized fire before the LORD. ⁶²The Levites enrolled were twenty-three thousand, every male one month or more of age. They were not enrolled with the other Israelites, however, for no heritage was given them among the Israelites.

⁶³These, then, were those enrolled by Moses and Eleazar the priest, when they enrolled the Israelites on the plains of Moab along the Jordan at Jericho. ⁶⁴Among them there was not one of those who had been enrolled by Moses and Aaron the priest, when they enrolled the Israelites in the wilderness of Sinai. ⁶⁵For the LORD had told them that they would surely die in the wilderness, and not one of them was left except Caleb, son of Je-phunneh, and Joshua, son of Nun.

27 Zelophehad's Daughters. ¹The daughters of Zelophehad, son of Hepher, son of Gilead, son of Machir, son of Manasseh, came forward. (Zelophe-had belonged to the clans of Manasseh,

---

and Mushi, sons of Merari (Exod 6:19; Num 3:20, 33); Korah, son of Izhar and grandson of Kohath (Exod 6:21).

The genealogy resumes with the line of Amram, son of Kohath. Amram married Jochebed, his father's sister (see Exod 6:20). Their children are the wilderness leaders: Aaron, Moses, and Miriam. The story of Aaron's sons, Nadab and Abihu, ends the genealogy. These two offered "unauthorized fire" (incense) before the Lord and they died (see Lev 10:1-2; Exod 30:9). They too are removed from the line of inheritance.

The chapter concludes with a summary: Moses and Eleazar took a census of the Israelites; no one remained of the previous generation except Caleb and Joshua (and, of course, Moses himself).

27:1-4 Zelophehad's daughters

Zelophehad had no sons, as was already noted in the previous chapter. Thus, according to the prevailing custom, he had no heirs; his claim to the land was lost. His five daughters, however, did not want their father's name to disappear. In the presence of the whole community at the tent of meeting, they make a direct appeal to those in authority, Moses, Eleazar, and the tribal leaders. Their appeal is simple and straightforward; they state the situation and make their request. Zelophehad has died, not because he participated in Korah's rebellion but because he was part of the generation that refused to enter the Promised Land at Caleb's urging (Num 14:1-35).

son of Joseph.) The names of his daughters were Mahlah, Noah, Hoglah, Milcah and Tirzah. ²Standing before Moses, Eleazar the priest, the princes, and the whole community at the entrance of the tent of meeting, they said: ³"Our father died in the wilderness. Although he did not join the faction of those who conspired against the LORD, Korah's faction, he died for his own sin without leaving any sons. ⁴But why should our father's name be cut off from his clan merely because he had no son? Give us land among our father's kindred."

Their protest suggests that, if Zelophehad had been a member of Korah's faction, his land would have been forfeit under the law of *herem*. The land (along with all the other possessions) of those condemned to capital punishment was turned over to the priests (see Commentary on 18:8-20) or to the king (see 1 Kgs 21:13-16). Zelophehad's death as a member of his generation is not the main problem, however; the problem is that he has no sons. His daughters object that his name will be "cut off" from his clan, just as the names of those who were guilty of rebellion or sacrilege: Dathan, Abiram, Korah, Nadab, and Abihu. Their proposed solution is simple: Allow daughters to inherit if there are no sons.

Several elements in this story are noteworthy. First of all, the daughters are allowed to speak in the presence of the assembly gathered at the cultic site, the tent of meeting. They are not required to transmit their request through a man. Second, the request they make is for a woman's right to inherit. The request is limited to an extraordinary situation and will be further limited in chapter 36; nonetheless, it demonstrates that women could be considered as legal persons in the community. Third, however, their proposed solution will affect only one generation. The land the daughters inherit will subsequently be inherited by their sons, who will be counted not in the clan of their mother but in the clan of their father. This situation will be addressed in chapter 36.

The daughters of Zelophehad are all named, a fact to be noted since only six to eight percent of the persons given names in the whole Bible are women. Some of their names also appear as the names of cities or territories in the central highlands, the area of the northern kingdom. In the Samaria Ostraca, an eighth-century record from Samaria reporting the arrival of wine and oil from several territories, Hoglah and Noah are named as two of the territories. Hoglah is near Geba and Noah is near Socoh. (The Samaria Ostraca also names some of the men mentioned as Manassite in the previous chapter: Iezer, Asriel, Shechem, and Shemida; see Num 26:29-32.) Tirzah is an important city in the territory of Manasseh; it is the capital of

Laws Concerning Heiresses. ⁵So Moses laid their case before the LORD, ⁶and the LORD said to him: ⁷The plea of Zelophehad's daughters is just; you shall give them hereditary land among their father's kindred and transfer their father's heritage to them. ⁸Tell the Israelites: If a man dies without leaving a son, you shall transfer his heritage to his daughter; ⁹if he has no daughter, you shall give his heritage to his brothers; ¹⁰if he has no brothers, you shall give his heritage to his father's brothers; ¹¹if his father had no brothers, you shall give his heritage to his nearest relative in his clan, who shall then take possession of it.

This will be the statutory procedure for the Israelites, as the LORD commanded Moses.

Joshua to Succeed Moses. ¹²The LORD said to Moses: Go up into this mountain of the Abarim range and view the land

---

the northern kingdom from the time of Jeroboam until Omri built Samaria (ca. 922–870 B.C.; see 1 Kgs 14:17; 15:21, 33; 16:6, 8, 9, 15, 17, 23). The beauty of the beloved in the Song of Songs is compared to Jerusalem and Tirzah (Song 6:4). This echo of their names shows another consequence of their request: the establishment of part of the tribe of Manasseh in the territory west of the Jordan. The Manassite clans of Machir and Gilead settled east of the Jordan in the area of Gilead and Bashan, the territory they claimed before the people crossed the Jordan (see Num 32:29-42; 34:13-15; Deut 3:12-17). But Manasseh was also given ten shares west of the Jordan because the daughters of Zelophehad each received a portion along with Manasseh's sons (Josh 17:1-6).

27:5-11 Laws concerning heiresses

The request of the daughters of Zelophehad leads to a change in the law of inheritance. Just as he had done in other cases for which there were no legal provisions (e.g., making arrangements for those unable to celebrate Passover at the prescribed time, 9:6-14; determining the punishment for breaking the sabbath, 15:32-36), Moses takes the daughters' request to the Lord.

The Lord validates the request and instructs Moses to add these specifications to the law: In the case of a man who dies without sons, a daughter has first right of inheritance, followed by male relatives in order of relationship: brothers, uncles, and then the next relative in line. The basic principle that men inherit still holds, but, at least in one situation, women also have property rights.

27:12-23 Joshua to succeed Moses

None of the exodus generation will enter the Promised Land except Caleb and Joshua. The transfer of priestly leadership has already taken place:

that I have given to the Israelites. ¹³When you have viewed it, you will be gathered to your people, as was Aaron your brother. ¹⁴For in the rebellion of the community in the wilderness of Zin you both rebelled against my order to acknowledge my holiness before them by means of the water. (These were the waters of Meribah of Kadesh in the wilderness of Zin.)

¹⁵Then Moses said to the LORD, ¹⁶"May the LORD, the God of the spirits of all humanity, set over the community someone ¹⁷who will be their leader in battle and who will lead them out and bring them in, that the LORD's community may not be like sheep without a shepherd." ¹⁸And the LORD replied to Moses: Take Joshua, son of Nun, a man

---

Eleazar has succeeded Aaron (20:25-29). The transfer of civil leadership from Moses to his successor must still be arranged. (The third wilderness leader, Miriam, has no successor.) Moses has already been told that he will die with the rest of his generation because of his own infidelity at the waters of Meribah (Num 20:7-13). So he prays that the Lord will appoint a new leader for the people who will be both mighty in battle and wise in leadership. He calls upon the Lord as "the God of the spirits of all humanity." Moses and Aaron addressed God by this same title when they appealed for mercy during Korah's rebellion (16:22). Now Moses is appealing to God's compassion that the people not be left as sheep without a shepherd.

God responds with instructions for a ritual to appoint Joshua as Moses' successor. Joshua is an ideal candidate. He is "a man of spirit," a charismatic leader like Joseph (see Gen 41:38). He was victorious in the first battle of the wilderness journey (Exod 17:8-16). He stayed on Mount Sinai with Moses for forty days and nights (Exod 24:12-18). He is devoted to God, remaining in the tent of meeting when Moses leaves (Exod 33:11). In his objection to the prophesying of Eldad and Medad he is perhaps over-protective of Moses' rights or of following proper procedure, but he accepts Moses' rebuke (Num 11:28-29). According to the Priestly tradition he is one of the two scouts to give a positive report and encourage the people to go up and take the Promised Land (Num 13:16; 14:6-10). Thus he is one of the two from the exodus generation who will enter the land (14:29-30, 38).

In the presence of the priest Eleazar and the whole community, Moses is to lay hands upon Joshua. Thus he will convey some of his own power and dignity (Hebrew *hod*) on Joshua just as some of his spirit was given to the seventy elders (Num 11:25). This is the only occurrence of *hod* in the Pentateuch; the word appears most often in the Psalms (8x) and is usually applied to God (Pss 8:2; 96:6; 104:1; 111:3; 145:5; 148:13). The Lord confers this majesty on the king (Ps 21:6; see Ps 45:4). Thus Joshua is greatly honored.

of spirit, and lay your hand upon him. [19]Have him stand before Eleazar the priest and the whole community, and commission him in their sight. [20]Invest him with some of your own power, that the whole Israelite community may obey him. [21]He shall present himself to Eleazar the priest, who will seek for him the decision of the Urim in the LORD's presence; and as it directs, Joshua, all the Israelites with him, and the whole community will go out for battle; and as it directs, they will come in.

[22]Moses did as the LORD had commanded him. Taking Joshua and having him stand before Eleazar the priest and the whole community, [23]he laid his hands on him and commissioned him, as the LORD had directed through Moses.

28 **General Sacrifices.** [1]The LORD said to Moses: [2]Give the Israelites this commandment: At their prescribed

---

Joshua will not be the sole leader of the people, however. He is dependent on the priest Eleazar to inform him of the Lord's decisions, especially regarding when to go into battle. Eleazar will seek these divine decisions by means of the Urim (the Thummim is undoubtedly also meant even though it is not mentioned here). These objects are mentioned only seven times in the Old Testament (Exod 28:30; Lev 8:8; Num 27:21; Deut 33:8; 1 Sam 28:6; Ezra 2:63; and Neh 7:65) and are never described. They seem to be two small objects, probably stones, which could either be cast on the ground or drawn out of a vessel. The two stones can be distinguished from each other and one side of each stone indicates "yes" and one side indicates "no." When cast, if the two show the same side, the Lord's answer is a definite "yes" or "no." If one shows "yes" and the other "no," the answer is inconclusive. When drawn out, the Urim indicates "yes" and the Thummim "no" (see 1 Sam 14:41).

At the end of his life Saul complains that he gets no answer from the Lord by the use of Urim and Thummim (1 Sam 28:6). It is likely that the Urim and Thummim were cast as a way of determining the guilty party when a battle was lost (Josh 7:14; 1 Sam 14:36-44), of deciding who will lead an attack (Judg 1:1-3; 20:17-18; see 2 Sam 5:23-24), in selecting Saul as king (1 Sam 10:20-22), and for any other decision requiring a "yes" or "no" answer (see 1 Sam 23:7-13; 2 Sam 2:1-2). They are carried in a pocket of the ephod, a priestly vestment (Exod 28:30; Lev 8:8).

The conclusion is typical of the Priestly tradition: Moses did exactly as God had commanded him.

28:1-2 General sacrifices

Chapters 28–29 outline procedures for offering the appropriate sacrifices throughout the year, beginning with the daily offering and ending with the yearly festivals. The primary audience is thus the priests who will be

times, you will be careful to present to me the food offerings that are due me, oblations of pleasing aroma to me.

Each Morning and Evening. ³You will tell them therefore: This is the oblation which you will offer to the LORD: two unblemished yearling lambs each day as the regular burnt offering, ⁴offering one lamb in the morning and the other during the evening twilight, ⁵each with a grain offering of one tenth of an ephah of bran flour mixed with a fourth of a hin of oil of crushed olives. ⁶This is the regular burnt offering that was made at Mount Sinai for a pleasing aroma, an oblation to the LORD. ⁷And as the libation for the first lamb, you will make a libation to the LORD in the sanctuary of a fourth of a hin of strong drink. ⁸The other lamb you will offer during the evening twilight, making the same grain offering and the same libation as in the morning, as an oblation of pleasing aroma to the LORD.

On the Sabbath. ⁹On the sabbath ▶ day: two unblemished yearling lambs,

---

offering the sacrifices. The first seven chapters of Numbers were concerned with the place where sacrifice should be offered. These chapters prescribe the time and the material for the offering. These offerings are to be burned so that their aroma may rise to the Lord.

28:3-8 Each morning and evening

The first sacrifice to be described is the regular daily offering (Hebrew *tamid*). The same offering is to be made both morning and evening: one male yearling lamb with the amount of grain and oil established in 15:4. A libation of strong drink is to be poured out with each lamb also according to the amount named in 15:5. The reason for the legislation is said to begin at Sinai although there is no mention of such a daily sacrifice there. Even after the temple is built, the daily sacrifice of a lamb seems to have occurred only in the morning with a grain offering in the evening (see 2 Kgs 16:15; Ezek 46:13-15). Only postexilic texts—the Priestly tradition in the Pentateuch and the Chronicler—describe animal sacrifice in the evening as well as in the morning (Exod 29:38-39; 1 Chr 16:40; 2 Chr 31:3).

The tradition of morning and evening prayer, however, is ancient. Offerings are made to God in the morning in thanksgiving for a new day and in petition for blessings on the work of the day; offerings are made in the evening in thanksgiving for the blessings of the day and repentance for faults committed as well as for protection from evil throughout the night.

28:9-10 On the sabbath

Other sacrifices are to be offered on special days, but these special sacrifices do not replace the daily offering. The daily sacrifice of a lamb morning with a grain offering of two tenths of an ephah of bran flour mixed with oil, and its libation. ¹⁰This is the sabbath burnt offering each sabbath, in addition to the regular burnt offering and its libation.

At the New Moon Feast. ¹¹On your new moons you will offer as a burnt offering to the LORD two bulls of the herd, one ram, and seven unblemished yearling lambs, ¹²with three tenths of an ephah of bran flour mixed with oil as the grain offering for each bull, two tenths of an ephah of bran flour mixed with oil as the grain offering for the ram, ¹³and one tenth of an ephah of bran flour

mixed with oil as the grain offering for each lamb, a burnt offering with a pleasing aroma, an oblation to the LORD. ¹⁴Their libations will consist of a half a hin of wine for each bull, a third of a hin for the ram, and a fourth of a hin for each lamb. This is the burnt offering for the new moon, for every new moon through the months of the year. ¹⁵Moreover, there will be one goat for a purification offering to the LORD; it will be offered in addition to the regular burnt offering and its libation.

At the Passover. ¹⁶The fourteenth day of the first month is the Passover of the

---

and evening must continue unabated. On the sabbath day two additional lambs are offered with the same accompanying grain, oil, and strong drink. In no other sabbath legislation in the Pentateuch is a sacrifice mentioned. The emphasis is always on refraining from work (see Exod 16:29-30; 20:8-11; 31:13-16; 35:2-3; Lev 23:3; Num 15:32-36; Deut 5:12-15). Besides this passage in Numbers only Ezekiel and 2 Chronicles mention sacrifice on the sabbath (Ezek 46:4; 2 Chr 31:3).

28:11-15 At the new moon feast

Months in Israel's calendar began at the new moon. The sacrifice to be offered at the beginning of each month (in addition to the regular daily sacrifice) consists of two bulls, one ram, and seven yearling lambs, each with the amount of grain, oil, and wine established in 15:1-12. A further offering of a male goat is required for a purification offering. This purification sacrifice was probably offered first as a way of atoning for any inadvertent failings of the people during the last month. Then the sacrifice for the new month was offered.

28:16-25 At the Passover

The focus in this passage is not on the Passover celebration itself, which is a family celebration (see Exod 12:1-11), but on the sacrifices to be offered during the Festival of Unleavened Bread during the seven days after Passover. These two feasts originated separately: Unleavened Bread is a harvest festival, celebrating the new grain that is as yet unleavened.

LORD, [17]and the fifteenth day of this month is the pilgrimage feast. For seven days unleavened bread is to be eaten. [18]On the first day you will declare a holy day, and you shall do no heavy work. [19]You will offer an oblation, a burnt offering to the LORD: two bulls of the herd, one ram, and seven yearling lambs that you are sure are unblemished. [20]Their grain offerings will be of bran flour mixed with oil; you will offer three tenths of an ephah for each bull and two tenths for the ram. [21]You will offer one tenth for each of the seven lambs; [22]and one goat as a purification offering to make atonement for yourselves. [23]These offerings you will make in addition to the morning burnt offering which is part of the regular burnt offering. [24]You will make exactly the same offerings each day for seven days as food offerings, oblations of pleasing aroma to the LORD; they will be offered in addition to the regular burnt offering with its libation. [25]On the seventh day you will declare a holy day: you shall do no heavy work.

At Pentecost. [26]On the day of first fruits, on your feast of Weeks, when you

Passover is related to nomadic rituals for protecting the flock during the move from winter to summer pasture. Legislation such as this is a reminder that the two feasts are separate even though they are celebrated at the same time.

The first day of the Festival of Unleavened Bread is a pilgrimage feast (Hebrew *hag*; see Exod 13:6; 23:15; 34:18; Lev 23:6). Before the seventh century B.C. the people could congregate at any sacred site to celebrate the feast. Josiah, however, decreed that the only legitimate place for sacrifice was the temple, so if they wished to participate, pilgrims were required to travel to Jerusalem. In addition to the sacred assembly, no heavy work is to be done. The sacrifice to be offered each day for seven days includes two bulls, one ram, and seven yearling lambs with the appropriate offerings of grain, oil, and the libation of wine or other strong drink. On the first day a goat is also to be sacrificed as a purification offering. The seventh day is a holy day on which heavy work is prohibited.

28:26-31 At Pentecost

The feast of Weeks, also called first fruits, celebrates the wheat harvest. Its time is determined by counting seven weeks (or seven sabbaths) after the barley harvest, celebrated at Passover (see Exod 34:22; Lev 23:15; Deut 16:9-10). The feast of Weeks was called Pentecost in Greek because of the fifty days (Greek *pentekonta*) between Passover and Weeks. The sacrifice for this feast (in addition to the regular daily offering) is the same as that for the seven days of Unleavened Bread. It includes two bulls, one ram, and seven yearling lambs with their offerings of grain

present to the LORD an offering of new grain, you will declare a holy day: you shall do no heavy work. ²⁷You will offer burnt offering for a pleasing aroma to the LORD: two bulls of the herd, one ram, and seven yearling lambs that you are sure are unblemished. ²⁸Their grain offerings will be of bran flour mixed with oil: three tenths of an ephah for each bull, two tenths for the ram, ²⁹and one tenth for each of the seven lambs. ³⁰One goat will be for a purification offering to make atonement for yourselves. ³¹You will make these offerings, together with their libations, in addition to the regular burnt offering with its grain offering.

29 **On New Year's Day.** ¹In the seventh month on the first day you will declare a holy day, and do no heavy work; it shall be a day on which you sound the trumpet. ²You will offer a burnt offering for a pleasing aroma to the LORD: one bull of the herd, one ram, and seven unblemished yearling lambs. ³Their grain offerings will be of bran flour mixed with oil: three tenths of an ephah for the bull, two tenths for the ram, ⁴and one tenth for each of the seven lambs. ⁵One goat will be a purification offering to make atonement for yourselves. ⁶These are in addition to the burnt offering for the new moon with its grain offering, and in addition to the regular burnt offering with its grain offering, together with the libations prescribed for them, for a pleasing aroma, an oblation to the LORD.

and oil and the libation of strong drink. A goat is to be offered also as a purification offering.

29:1-6 On New Year's Day

Three celebrations are held during the seventh month: the New Year on the first day, the Day of Atonement on the tenth day, and Booths on the fifteenth day. New Year's Day is announced with trumpet blasts; it is a holy day on which no heavy work may be done (see Lev 23:24). The sacrifices to be offered are: one bull, one ram, and seven yearling lambs with their grain and oil and presumably with the libation of wine also. The purification sacrifice of a male goat is also to be offered.

It may seem odd to name the first day of the seventh month "New Year's Day." Two calendars were in effect during the biblical period. In one calendar the year began in the spring. Nisan, the month of Passover, was the first month (see Exod 12:2). In the other calendar followed by the Babylonians but also represented by the tenth-century Gezer calendar, the year began in the fall. The Jewish New Year, Rosh Hashanah, is still celebrated on this autumn day even though Nisan continues to be called the first month. Compare this to the Christian practice of designating the First Sunday of Advent as the beginning of the liturgical year even though it falls during the eleventh or twelfth month of the civil calendar.

On the Day of Atonement. ⁷On the tenth day of this seventh month you will declare a holy day, humble yourselves, and do no sort of work. ⁸You will offer a burnt offering to the LORD, a pleasing aroma: one bull of the herd, one ram, and seven yearling lambs that you are sure are unblemished. ⁹Their grain offerings of bran flour mixed with oil: three tenths of an ephah for the bull, two tenths for the one ram, ¹⁰and one tenth for each of the seven lambs. ¹¹One goat will be a purification offering. These are in addition to the purification offering for purging, the regular burnt offering with its grain offering, and their libations.

On the Feast of Booths. ¹²On the fifteenth day of the seventh month you will declare a holy day: you shall do no heavy work. For the following seven days you will celebrate a pilgrimage feast to the LORD. ¹³You will offer a burnt offering, an oblation of pleasing aroma to the LORD: thirteen bulls of the herd, two rams, and fourteen yearling lambs that are unblemished. ¹⁴Their grain offerings will be of bran flour mixed with oil: three tenths of an ephah for each of the thirteen bulls, two tenths for each of

29:7-11 On the Day of Atonement

Just as the first day of the seventh month is not specifically named "New Year's" in the previous verses, so the tenth day is not specifically named "Day of Atonement" here (Hebrew *yom kippur*). It is so named elsewhere, however (Lev 23:27-28; 25:9), and is clearly signified by the additional instruction to "humble oneself," which frequently indicates fasting (see Isa 58:3, 5; Ps 35:13). The celebratory sacrifice consists of one bull, one ram, and seven yearling lambs with their grain and oil (and, no doubt, the libation of wine). In addition to the customary goat sacrificed as a purification offering, a bull is also offered as a purification offering for the tent of meeting (see Lev 16:11-12). The full legislation for the Day of Atonement is found in Leviticus 16.

29:12–30:1 On the Feast of Booths

The Feast of Booths (Sukkoth) is the third harvest festival (along with Passover and Weeks) in the calendar. It is sometimes called "Ingathering" (Hebrew *ʾasiph*; Exod 23:16; 34:22) because of the harvest of fruits (mostly grapes and figs) and nuts in the fall of the year. It is a pilgrimage feast and a holy day on which no heavy work may be done. It is sometimes called *the* festival, indicating its importance (1 Kgs 8:2, 65; 12:32; Ezek 45:25; 2 Chr 5:3; 7:8-9; see Ps 81:4). The number of animals sacrificed during the seven days of celebration also demonstrates the significance of this feast. Every day for seven days two rams and fourteen yearling lambs are sacrificed along with a goat for a purification offering.

the two rams, [15]and one tenth for each of the fourteen lambs. [16]One goat will be a purification offering. These are in addition to the regular burnt offering with its grain offering and libation.

[17]On the second day: twelve bulls of the herd, two rams, and fourteen unblemished yearling lambs, [18]with the grain offerings and libations for the bulls, rams and lambs in their prescribed number, [19]as well as one goat as a purification offering, besides the regular burnt offering with its grain offering and libation.

[20]On the third day: eleven bulls, two rams, and fourteen unblemished yearling lambs, [21]with the grain offerings and libations for the bulls, rams and lambs in their prescribed number, [22]as well as one goat for a purification offering, besides the regular burnt offering with its grain offering and libation.

[23]On the fourth day: ten bulls, two rams, and fourteen unblemished yearling lambs, [24]the grain offerings and liba-tions for the bulls, rams and lambs in their prescribed number, [25]as well as one goat as a purification offering, besides the regular burnt offering, its grain offering and libation.

[26]On the fifth day: nine bulls, two rams, and fourteen unblemished yearling lambs, [27]with the grain offerings and libations for the bulls, rams and lambs in their prescribed number, [28]as well as one goat as a purification offering, besides the regular burnt offering with its grain offering and libation.

[29]On the sixth day: eight bulls, two rams, and fourteen unblemished yearling lambs, [30]with the grain offerings and libations for the bulls, rams and lambs in their prescribed number, [31]as well as one goat as a purification offering, besides the regular burnt offering, its grain offering and libation.

[32]On the seventh day: seven bulls, two rams, and fourteen unblemished yearling lambs, [33]with the grain offerings and libations for the bulls, rams and

On the first day thirteen bulls are also sacrificed, on the second day twelve bulls, on the third day eleven bulls, and so on. On the seventh day seven bulls are sacrificed along with the two rams and fourteen lambs, making a grand total of seventy bulls as well as fourteen rams, ninety-eight lambs, and seven goats for purification offerings. The number seven signifies completion, so the seven bulls sacrificed on the seventh day to make a total of seventy bulls emphasize the fullness of the offering. It is not quite enough, however. On the eighth day (one past the perfect number) at a public assembly, one final sacrifice is offered: one bull, one ram, seven yearling lambs with their grain and oil and libations, along with one male goat for a purification offering. Throughout these eight days the regular sacrifice of one lamb in the morning and one lamb in the evening has also been offered daily. As usual, the Priestly tradition assures us that Moses followed the Lord's instructions exactly.

Israelites in the wilderness receiving manna from heaven, ca. 15th century

lambs in their prescribed number, ³⁴as well as one goat as a purification offering, besides the regular burnt offering, its grain offering and libation.

³⁵On the eighth day you will hold a public assembly: you shall do no heavy work. ³⁶You will offer a burnt offering, an oblation of pleasing aroma to the LORD: one bull, one ram, and seven unblemished yearling lambs, ³⁷with the grain offerings and libations for the bulls, rams and lambs in their prescribed number, ³⁸as well as one goat as a purification offering, besides the regular burnt offering with its grain offering and libation.

³⁹These are the offerings you will make to the LORD on your festivals, besides your votive or voluntary offerings of burnt offerings, grain offerings, libations, and communion offerings.

30 ¹So Moses instructed the Israelites exactly as the LORD had commanded him.

Validity and Annulment of Vows. ²Moses said to the heads of the Israelite tribes, "This is what the LORD has commanded: ³When a man makes a vow to the LORD or binds himself under oath to a pledge, he shall not violate his word, but must fulfill exactly the promise he has uttered.

⁴"When a woman makes a vow to the LORD, or binds herself to a pledge, while still in her father's house in her youth, ⁵and her father learns of her vow or the pledge to which she bound herself and says nothing to her about it, then any vow or any pledge to which she bound herself remains valid. ⁶But if on the day he learns of it her father opposes her, then any vow or any pledge to which

---

30:2-17 Validity and annulment of vows

Two types of voluntary obligations are treated in this chapter: a vow (Hebrew *neder*), which is a promise to offer something to God if God first grants a request; a pledge (Hebrew *ʾissar*, literally "a binding"), which is a promise either to do something or refrain from doing something (e.g., to fast). Sometimes the pledge is confirmed by an oath (Hebrew *shebuʿah*). The chapter begins with the flat statement that men are obligated to pay their vows or fulfill their pledges.

But the point of the chapter is the placement of restrictions on women who make such vows or pledges. Women had the freedom to make these promises voluntarily. Since these promises most frequently involved the gift of real property, however, the means to fulfill them usually depended on the willingness of whichever male figure had legal control of the woman: her father or her husband. (See Lev 27 for legislation regarding the payment of vows.) The only women who had free control of their property were widows, divorced women, or prostitutes.

If an unmarried woman still in her father's house makes a vow or pledge, her father has two choices (vv. 4-6). He may either approve her

she bound herself becomes invalid; and the LORD will release her from it, since her father opposed her.

⁷"If she marries while under a vow or under a rash pledge to which she bound herself, ⁸and her husband learns of it, yet says nothing to her on the day he learns it, then the vows or the pledges to which she bound herself remain valid. ⁹But if on the day her husband learns of it he opposes her, he thereby annuls the vow she had made or the rash pledge to which she had bound herself, and the LORD will release her from it. ¹⁰(The vow of a widow or of a divorced woman, however, any pledge to which such a woman binds herself, is valid.)

¹¹"If it is in her husband's house that she makes a vow or binds herself under oath to a pledge, ¹²and her husband learns of it yet says nothing to her to oppose her, then all her vows remain valid or any pledge to which she has bound herself. ¹³But if on the day he learns of them her husband annuls them, then whatever she has expressly promised in her vows or in her pledge becomes invalid; since her husband has annulled them, the LORD will release her from them.

¹⁴"Any vow or any pledge that she makes under oath to humble herself, her husband may either confirm or annul. ¹⁵But if her husband, day after day, says

---

action by remaining silent or immediately refuse to allow her to make such a promise, in which case her vow or pledge is invalid. If her father remains silent, he is liable for payment, possibly an animal for sacrifice. If he opposes her promise, then neither the father nor the young woman is obligated. She is released from her vow or pledge because she has no power to fulfill it.

A husband has the same options and obligations if his wife makes a vow or a pledge (vv. 11-13). Other conditions also apply (vv. 7-9). If a woman is already obligated to fulfill a vow or a pledge when she marries, her husband has the power to annul it immediately even though her father presumably approved it. But in either case—whether the woman had made the promise before or after marriage—if the husband delays and remains silent, then he takes on the obligation to supply the means for fulfilling the promise. He cannot annul her commitments at a later time; he is responsible for either making the payment or bearing the guilt of an unfulfilled vow or pledge.

A woman who is not under the legal control of a man, such as a widow or divorced woman, bears the obligation for her own vows and pledges just as a man does (v. 10). Perhaps her husband approved her vow before he divorced her or died. Now she bears the responsibility alone. This situation may place a serious burden on the woman, since she has few economic resources. The third circumstance in which a woman is independent is that of a prostitute. That situation is not mentioned here, but Deuteronomy

nothing at all to her, he thereby confirms all her vows or all the pledges incumbent upon her; he has confirmed them, because on the day he learned of them he said nothing to her. ¹⁶If, however, he annuls them some time after he first learned of them, he will be responsible for her guilt."

¹⁷These are the statutes which the LORD commanded Moses concerning a husband and his wife, as well as a father and his daughter while she is still in her youth in her father's house.

31 Campaign Against the Midianites. ¹The LORD said to Moses: ²Avenge the Israelites on the Midianites, and then you will be gathered to your people. ³So Moses told the people, "Arm some men among you for the campaign, to attack Midian and to execute the

---

specifically forbids the payment of a vow with resources gained through prostitution (Deut 23:19; see Prov 7:14).

There are not many examples of women making vows or binding themselves to a pledge. Hannah makes a vow to God: If God gives her a son, she will give him back to God as a Nazirite serving in the sanctuary (1 Sam 1:11). The Nazirite vow itself is open to both men and women (Num 6:2). Lemuel's mother calls him the "son of my vows," suggesting that she too promised to offer something to God if God gave her a son (Prov 31:2). Jeremiah complains that both men and women are fulfilling their vows to offer something to the "queen of heaven," probably the goddess Astarte. For either a man or a woman the fulfillment of a vow is a serious matter. Qoheleth advises, "It is better not to make a vow than make it and not fulfill it" (Eccl 5:4; see Prov 20:25).

31:1-12 Campaign against the Midianites

Chapter 31 begins where chapter 25 left off, with the Lord's command to crush the Midianites because of the incident at Baal Peor (25:16-17). Moses is warned that this is virtually his last task. The people are almost ready to enter the Promised Land and he will not go with them.

The purposes of the Priestly writers in telling the story of this battle are two: to explain why the previously friendly Midianites become enemies after the Israelites enter the Promised Land, and to outline the customs for holy war. First of all, what happened with the Midianites? They are identified as the descendants of Abraham through his third wife, Keturah (Gen 25:1-2, 4). Moses lived with the Midianite priest Reuel (also known as Jethro) when he fled from Pharaoh; Reuel's daughter Zipporah became his wife and saved his life (Exod 2:15-22; 4:24-26). Moses even invited his brother-in-law Hobab to accompany Israel on its march through the wilderness (Num 10:29-31).

LORD's vengeance on Midian. ⁴From each of the tribes of Israel you will send a thousand men to the campaign." ⁵From the contingents of Israel, therefore, a thousand men of each tribe were levied, so that there were twelve thousand men armed for war. ⁶Moses sent them out on the campaign, a thousand from each tribe, with Phinehas, son of Eleazar, the priest for the campaign, who had with him the sacred vessels and the trumpets for sounding the alarm. ⁷They waged war against the Midianites, as the LORD had commanded Moses, and killed every male. ⁸Besides those slain in battle, they killed the kings of Midian: Evi, Rekem, Zur, Hur and Reba, the five kings of Midian; and they also killed Balaam, son of Beor, with the sword. ⁹But the Israelites took captive the women of the Midianites with their children, and all their herds and flocks and wealth as loot, ¹⁰while they set on fire all the towns where they had settled and all their encampments. ¹¹Then they took all the plunder, with the people and animals they had captured, and brought the captives, together with the spoils and plunder, ¹²to Moses and Eleazar the priest and to the Israelite community at their camp on the plains of Moab by the Jordan opposite Jericho.

The situation turned when Midian joined with Balak in attempting to curse Israel (Num 22:4, 7) and when Zimri brought a Midianite woman into the camp in the midst of the Baal Peor incident (Num 25:6-15). Perhaps the Priestly authors have inserted Midian into these events in order to explain how they became a mortal enemy when Israel was settling the land. They remained a problem in the time of the judges when God raised up Gideon to free Israel from their power (Judg 6:1–8:28; see Ps 83:10; Isa 9:3).

Second, the Priestly writers use this battle as a model for the conquest of the land and an example of how to fight a holy war. When Moses musters the troops, a thousand men from each tribe, to attack Midian, there is no mention of a general, not even Joshua. The troops are accompanied by the priest Phinehas who has the sacred vessels and the trumpets with him. The "sacred vessel" is probably the ark of the covenant, symbolizing God's presence with Israel in the battle (see Num 10:35-36; 1 Sam 4:1-3). The trumpets are used to sound the alarm (see Num 10:1-10).

Israel goes to war under God's command. The amazingly successful result is what Israel can expect if they are faithful to God and do only what they are commanded to do. According to the narrator, all the Midianite men are killed including their five kings and Balaam, son of Beor. All the Midianite towns and encampments are burned. Everything the Midianites owned, including their women and children, are taken as spoil. All the spoil is brought to Moses and Eleazar the priest. Its disposition will also illustrate the customs of holy war.

Treatment of the Captives. ¹³When Moses and Eleazar the priest, with all the leaders of the community, went outside the camp to meet them, ¹⁴Moses became angry with the officers of the army, the commanders of thousands and the commanders of hundreds, who were returning from the military campaign. ¹⁵"So you have spared all the women!" he exclaimed. ¹⁶"These are the very ones who on Balaam's advice were behind the Israelites' unfaithfulness to the Lord in the affair at Peor, so that plague struck the Lord's community. ¹⁷Now kill, therefore, every male among the children and kill every woman who has had sexual relations with a man. ¹⁸But you may spare for yourselves all the girls who have not had sexual relations.

Purification After Combat. ¹⁹"Moreover, remain outside the camp for seven days; every one of you who has killed anyone or touched someone killed will purify yourselves on the third and on

31:13-18 Treatment of the captives

The rules for dealing with spoils are usually called *herem*, the ban or doom. The word is not used here, but the principles reflect the instruction in Deuteronomy 20–21. If the conquered enemy is within the Promised Land, everything is to be destroyed—all the people and all the property (Deut 20:16-18). Everything must be put under the ban lest Israel be led into worshiping other gods. If the conquered enemy is at a considerable distance, however, then only the men (perhaps also boys) must be killed; it is permissible to keep everything else—women, children, livestock, and anything else that is valuable (Deut 20:13-15). Captive women may be taken as wives after a period of mourning for their parents (Deut 21:10-14). The Midianites are not regarded as a people of the Promised Land, so the Israelites kill only the adult men.

Moses interprets the law more strictly, however. When he discovers that all the women have been spared, he is furious. He blames the Midianite women for the infidelity of Israel at Baal Peor and commands that only women who are virgins (including female children) be spared. All other captives—married women and boys—are to be killed. The virgins may be taken as wives. Apparently they are not seen as a threat to lead the people into idolatry.

31:19-24 Purification after combat

All those involved in the war—soldiers and captives—must go through a ritual of purification before they are allowed into the camp. Even if this is a holy war, killing and contact with the dead corrupt the participants. They must follow the ritual described in Numbers 19, using the purifying water prepared with the ashes of the red heifer. In addition, all material objects

the seventh day—both you and your captives. ²⁰You will also purify every garment, every article of leather, everything made of goats' hair, and every article of wood."

²¹Eleazar the priest told the soldiers who had taken part in the battle: "This is the prescribed ritual which the LORD has commanded Moses: ²²gold, silver, bronze, iron, tin and lead—²³whatever can stand fire—you shall put into the fire, that it may become clean; however, it must also be purified with water of purification. But whatever cannot stand fire you must put into the water. ²⁴On the seventh day you will wash your garments, and then you will again be clean. After that you may enter the camp."

Division of the Spoils. ²⁵The LORD said to Moses: ²⁶With the help of Eleazar the priest and of the heads of the ancestral houses of the community, inventory all the spoils captured, human being and beast alike; ²⁷then divide the spoils between the warriors who went on the campaign and the whole community. ²⁸You will levy a tax for the LORD on the soldiers who went on the campaign: one out of every five hundred persons, oxen, donkeys, and sheep. ²⁹From their half you will take it and give it to Eleazar the priest as a contribution to the LORD. ³⁰From the Israelites' half you will take one captive from every fifty human beings, oxen, donkeys, and sheep—all the animals—and give them to the Levites,

---

must be purified. Anything made of metal that can endure burning must be purified both by fire and with the water of purification. Other objects need only be cleansed with the water of purification.

31:25-31 Division of the spoils

Eleazar is again a major participant in the action as he was with the purification ritual. He and the ancestral leaders are commanded to inventory all the spoils and then divide them in half. Half will go to the soldiers and the other half will be divided among the rest of the community. This principle is explained later by David: "the share of the one who goes down to battle shall be the same as that of the one who remains with the baggage—they share alike" (1 Sam 30:24). The tax for the two groups is different, however. The soldiers are taxed at a rate of .2 percent; the people are taxed at a rate of 2 percent. The soldiers' tax is paid to Eleazar the priest and the sanctuary; the people's tax is paid to the Levites. This is consistent with another principle of *herem* that what is "doomed" is given to the sanctuary (Lev 27:21; Num 18:14).

31:32-47 Amount of the plunder

The staggering amount of plunder is also a clue that this story has been idealized. The pattern of the list is similar to that of Numbers 7. It seems to be an oral report from a table: oxen, 72,000; donkeys, 61,000; etc.

who perform the duties of the LORD's tabernacle. [31]So Moses and Eleazar the priest did this, as the LORD had commanded Moses.

Amount of the Plunder. [32]This plunder, what was left of the loot which the troops had taken, amounted to six hundred and seventy-five thousand sheep, [33]seventy-two thousand oxen, [34]sixty-one thousand donkeys, [35]and thirty-two thousand women who had not had sexual relations.

[36]The half-share that fell to those who had gone out on the campaign was in number: three hundred and thirty-seven thousand five hundred sheep, [37]of which six hundred and seventy-five fell as tax to the LORD; [38]thirty-six thousand oxen, of which seventy-two fell as tax to the LORD; [39]thirty thousand five hundred donkeys, of which sixty-one fell as tax to the LORD; [40]and sixteen thousand persons, of whom thirty-two persons fell as tax to the LORD. [41]Moses gave the taxes contributed to the LORD to Eleazar the priest, exactly as the LORD had commanded Moses.

[42]As for the Israelites' half, which Moses had taken from the men who had fought—[43]the community's half was three hundred and thirty-seven thousand five hundred sheep, [44]thirty-six thousand oxen, [45]thirty thousand five hundred donkeys, [46]and sixteen thousand persons. [47]From the Israelites' half, Moses took one captive from every fifty, from human being and beast alike, and gave them to the Levites, who performed the duties of the LORD's tabernacle, exactly as the LORD had commanded Moses.

Gifts of the Officers. [48]Then those who were officers over the contingents of the army, commanders of thousands and commanders of hundreds, came up to Moses [49]and said to him, "Your servants have counted the soldiers under our command, and not one of us is missing. [50]So, we have brought as an offering to the LORD articles of gold that each of us has picked up—anklets, bracelets, rings, earrings, or pendants—to make atonement for ourselves before the LORD." [51]Moses and Eleazar the priest accepted the gold from them, all fashioned pieces. [52]The gold that was given as a contribution to the LORD—from the commanders of thousands and the commanders of hundreds—amounted in all to sixteen thousand seven hundred and fifty shekels. [53]What the common soldiers had looted each one kept for

---

31:48-54 Gifts of the officers

The officers take a census of the soldiers and discover that not one soldier has fallen in the battle (one more clue that this story is idealized). From their plunder they bring articles of gold as a donation to the sanctuary. This offering is intended either as atonement or a ransom for their lives. Perhaps they need to make atonement because they have attacked and killed other human beings. Perhaps they need to pay a ransom because their lives now belong to God who has saved them all from death. The gold is put in the tent of meeting as a memorial, a reminder before God.

himself. [54]So Moses and Eleazar the priest accepted the gold from the commanders of thousands and of hundreds, and put it in the tent of meeting as a reminder on behalf of the Israelites before the LORD.

32 **Request of Gad and Reuben.** [1]Now the Reubenites and Gadites had a very large number of livestock. Noticing that the land of Jazer and of Gilead was a place suited to livestock, [2]the Gadites and Reubenites came to Moses and Eleazar the priest and to the leaders of the community and said,

[3]"The region of Ataroth, Dibon, Jazer, Nimrah, Heshbon, Elealeh, Sebam, Nebo and Baal-meon—[4]the land which the LORD has laid low before the community of Israel, is a land for livestock, and your servants have livestock." [5]They continued, "If we find favor with you, let this land be given to your servants as their possession. Do not make us cross the Jordan."

Moses' Rebuke. [6]But Moses answered the Gadites and Reubenites: "Are your kindred, then, to go to war, while you remain here? [7]Why do you

32:1-5 Request of Gad and Reuben

Three issues dominate chapter 32: the question of inheritance, specifically inheritance on the east side of the Jordan; the question of just how far the Promised Land extends; and the demands of holy war. The request of two tribes, Gad and Reuben, will have an impact on all three issues.

Representatives of these two tribes address the full leadership of Israel: Moses, the priest Eleazar, and the community leaders. The economy of these two tribes is based on shepherding and their desire is to remain in the good pastureland in Gilead on the east side of the Jordan, the land that was taken from the Amorite king Sihon (see Num 21:21-32). This land with its towns lies between the Arnon (the northern border of Moab) and the Jabbok. But their plea not to be forced to cross the Jordan implies that they do not want to participate in the battles necessary to wrest the land west of the Jordan from the Canaanites.

32:6-15 Moses' rebuke

Moses does not look favorably on their request. His first objection indicates that the land requested by Gad and Reuben is not the land the Lord has given the Israelites, and thus is not part of the Promised Land. He compares their intention to the action of the scouts whose unfavorable report prevented Israel from entering Canaan from the south (Num 13–14). Just as Israel begged to stay in the wilderness rather than face the "giants" of the scout's report, so now these two tribes plead to stay here rather than fight the Canaanites on the other side of the Jordan. Moses comes close to laying the primary blame for God's anger against the exodus generation

wish to discourage the Israelites from crossing to the land the LORD has given them? ⁸That is just what your ancestors did when I sent them from Kadesh-barnea to reconnoiter the land. ⁹They went up to the Wadi Eshcol and reconnoitered the land, then so discouraged the Israelites that they would not enter the land the LORD had given them. ¹⁰At that time the anger of the LORD flared up, and he swore: ¹¹None of the men twenty years old or more who have come up from Egypt will see the land I promised under oath to Abraham and Isaac and Jacob, because they have not followed me unreservedly—¹²except the Kenizzite Caleb, son of Jephunneh, the Kenizzite, and Joshua, son of Nun, since they have followed the LORD unreservedly. ¹³So the anger of the LORD flared up against the Israelites and he made them wander in the wilderness forty years, until the whole generation that had done evil in the sight of the LORD had disappeared. ¹⁴And now here

you are, offspring of sinful stock, rising up in your ancestors' place to add still more to the LORD's blazing anger against the Israelites. ¹⁵If you turn away from following him, he will again abandon them in the wilderness, and you will bring about the ruin of this entire people."

Counter Proposal. ¹⁶But they approached him and said: "We will only build sheepfolds here for our flocks and towns for our families; ¹⁷but we ourselves will march as troops in the vanguard before the Israelites, until we have led them to their destination. Meanwhile our families will remain in the fortified towns because of the land's inhabitants. ¹⁸We will not return to our homes until all the Israelites have taken possession of their heritage. ¹⁹But we will not claim any heritage with them across the Jordan and beyond, because we have received a heritage for ourselves on the eastern side of the Jordan."

on the Gadites and Reubenites, the "sinful stock" from which these tribes come. If their offspring persist in their refusal to cross the Jordan it will bring about the ruination of the whole people.

32:16-19 Counter proposal

The Gadites and Reubenites not only promise to cross the Jordan and fight, they volunteer to lead the charge. The question regarding holy war is thus answered: all the tribes must participate in the conquest of the Promised Land. Inheritance is a different matter, however. As security for their families and property, they propose to construct sheepfolds for their flocks and rebuild and fortify the towns east of the Jordan. They will not claim any heritage in the land west of the Jordan. They repeat their request to claim as their heritage the land east of the Jordan. Does this mean that they will live outside the Promised Land or is Transjordan also part of the Promised Land?

Agreement Reached. ²⁰Moses said to them in reply: "If you do this—if you march as troops before the LORD into battle ²¹and cross the Jordan in full force before the LORD until he has driven his enemies out of his way ²²and the land is subdued before the LORD, then you may return here, free from every obligation to the LORD and to Israel, and this land will be your possession before the LORD. ²³But if you do not do this, you will have sinned against the LORD, and you can be sure that the consequences of your sin will overtake you. ²⁴Build the towns, then, for your families, and the folds for your flocks, but fulfill what you have promised."

²⁵The Gadites and Reubenites answered Moses, "Your servants will do as my lord commands. ²⁶While our wives and children, our livestock and other animals remain there in the towns of

32:20-32 Agreement reached

Moses agrees to the proposal of the Gadites and Reubenites. If they march at the head of the troops and persevere until the land west of the Jordan is subdued, then they may return and claim the land east of the Jordan. If they fail to keep their promise, however, not only will that be a sin against the Lord but their sin will pursue them and they will never escape its consequences. The Gadites and Reubenites repeat their intention to keep their promise and fight for the land across the Jordan.

The question regarding the status of these two tribes and the land east of the Jordan is left ambiguous. They promised to march "before the Israelites" (v. 17) and they are told to march "before the LORD" (v. 21). Does this mean that the Lord is with Israel and, by implication, not with them? Or is the meaning simply that they will march in front of the ark of the covenant as they go into battle? In either case, they are separated from the rest of Israel. They are further told that if they keep their promise, they have no more obligation to the Lord or to Israel. Does this apply only to the taking of the land or is it a more permanent separation? In spite of the questions, the land in Transjordan is identified as their "possession before the LORD," which seems to indicate that they are still full members of Israel and that their land is part of what God had promised their ancestors.

Moses solemnizes the decision by commanding the two leaders who will lead the Jordan crossing, Eleazar the priest and Joshua the leader of the troops, to allow Gad and Reuben to inherit Gilead as long as they cross the Jordan with the rest of Israel to fight for the land. If, on the other hand, the two tribes fail in this commitment, they will be deprived of any holding east of the Jordan and will be forced to accept land with the rest of the tribes on the west side of the Jordan.

Gilead, [27]all your servants will go across as armed troops before the LORD to battle, just as my lord says."

[28]So Moses gave this command in their regard to Eleazar the priest, to Joshua, son of Nun, and to the heads of the ancestral houses of the Israelite tribes: [29]He said to them, "If all the Gadites and Reubenites cross the Jordan with you in full force before the LORD into battle, the land will be subdued before you, and you will give them Gilead as a possession. [30]But if they will not go across in force with you before the LORD, you will bring their wives and children and livestock across before you into Canaan, and they will possess a holding among you in the land of Canaan."

[31]To this the Gadites and Reubenites replied, "We will do what the LORD has ordered your servants. [32]We ourselves will go across in force before the LORD into the land of Canaan, but we will retain our hereditary property on this side of the Jordan." [33]So Moses gave them— the Gadites and Reubenites, as well as half the tribe of Manasseh, son of Joseph—the kingdom of Sihon, king of the Amorites, and the kingdom of Og, king of Bashan, the land with its towns, and the districts of the surrounding towns.

[34]The Gadites rebuilt the cities of Dibon, Ataroth, Aroer, [35]Atroth-shophan, Jazer, Jogbehah, [36]Beth-nimrah and Beth-haran—fortified cities—and sheepfolds. [37]The Reubenites rebuilt Heshbon, El-ealeh, Kiriathaim, [38]Nebo, Baal-meon (names to be changed!), and Sibmah. These towns, which they rebuilt, they called by their old names.

Other Conquests. [39]The descendants of Machir, son of Manasseh, went to Gilead and captured it, dispossessing the Amorites who were there. [40](Moses gave Gilead to Machir, son of Manasseh, and he settled there.) [41]Jair, a descendant of Manasseh, went and captured their tent villages, and called them Havvoth-jair. [42]Nobah went and captured Kenath with its dependencies and called it Nobah after his own name.

A third time the Gadites and Reubenites pledge to keep their promise (32:31-32; see 32:17-18, 25-27). Moses then officially designates the land taken from Sihon and Og as their heritage. A surprise in verse 33 is the assignment of part of this land to half the tribe of Manasseh. The heritage of Manasseh west of the Jordan has already been secured with the right of the daughters of Zelophehad to inherit their father's land (27:1-11). Other clans of Manasseh settled in northern Gilead and Bashan, territory taken from Og (21:33-35). The presence of all three tribes in Transjordan is legitimated by Moses' proclamation.

32:39-42 Other conquests

The story of the Manassite clans is expanded in these verses. The assignment of Transjordanian land to the clans of Machir and Jair is reported in Deuteronomy in greater detail (Deut 3:13-15).

137

33 **Stages of the Journey.** ¹The following are the stages by which the Israelites went out by companies from the land of Egypt under the guidance of Moses and Aaron. ²Moses recorded the starting points of the various stages at the direction of the LORD. These are the stages according to their starting points: ³They set out from Rameses in the first month, on the fifteenth day of the first month. On the day after the Passover the Israelites went forth in triumph, in view of all Egypt, ⁴while the Egyptians buried those whom the LORD had struck down, every firstborn; on their gods, too, the LORD executed judgments.

Israelite communities in Transjordan lasted from the settlement period until the Assyrian deportations began under Tiglath-Pileser III in 734 B.C. Their legitimacy as full participants in Israel continued to be questioned. Their building of an altar east of the Jordan leads to the threat of war (Josh 22:10-34). The confrontation is settled only by their assurance that no sacrifices will be offered on this altar. (The controversy may reflect the seventh-century designation of the Jerusalem temple as the only site where sacrifice may be offered; see Deut 12.) When the kingdoms divided in 922 B.C., the territory of Reuben, Gad, and Manasseh became part of the northern kingdom, Israel. Elijah the prophet was a Gileadite, from east of the Jordan. The Transjordan settlements flourished under Omri (876–869 B.C.) but came to an end with the final deportation when Samaria was conquered in 722 B.C.

33:1-4 Stages of the journey

These final chapters of Numbers set the stage for the crossing of the Jordan and the conquest of the Promised Land. Israel has been encamped on the plains of Moab since the victories over Sihon and Og (22:1). Matters of inheritance and regulations for worship in the land have predominated in chapters 26–32. Chapter 33 is a recapitulation of the journey from the exodus to the plains of Moab; the chapter concludes with orders for the taking over of Canaan. Israel is described as an army on the march, company by company. Only forty camping sites between Rameses, the point of origin, and the plains of Moab, the arrival point, are listed for the forty years. The journey can be divided into three sections: Egypt to Sinai, Sinai to Kadesh, Kadesh to the Plains of Moab. The itinerary is written down by Moses. Besides writing down the law (Exod 24:4; 34:27; Deut 31:9, 24) the only writing Moses is said to have done is the curse against Amalek (Exod 17:14), his final song (Deut 31:22), and this itinerary.

The exodus is presented as a great victory of the Lord over the Egyptians and their gods (Exod 12:12). Israel leaves, not secretly as in the pre-Priestly tradition (Exod 12:37-39), but in full view of all Egypt (Exod 13:18).

From Egypt to Sinai. [5]Setting out from Rameses, the Israelites camped at Succoth. [6]Setting out from Succoth, they camped at Etham near the edge of the wilderness. [7]Setting out from Etham, they turned back to Pi-hahiroth, which is opposite Baal-zephon, and they camped opposite Migdol. [8]Setting out from Pi-hahiroth, they crossed over through the sea into the wilderness, and after they traveled a three days' journey in the wilderness of Etham, they camped at Marah. [9]Setting out from Marah, they came to Elim; at Elim there were twelve springs of water and seventy palm trees, and they camped there. [10]Setting out from Elim, they camped beside the Red Sea. [11]Setting out from the Red Sea, they camped in the wilderness of Sin. [12]Setting out from the wilderness of Sin, they camped at Dophkah. [13]Setting out from Dophkah, they camped at Alush. [14]Setting out from Alush, they camped at Rephidim, where there was no water for the people to drink. [15]Setting out from Rephidim, they camped in the wilderness of Sinai.

From Sinai to Kadesh. [16]Setting out from the wilderness of Sinai, they camped at Kibroth-hattaavah. [17]Setting out from Kibroth-hattaavah, they camped at Hazeroth. [18]Setting out from Hazeroth, they camped at Rithmah. [19]Setting out from Rithmah, they camped at Rimmon-perez. [20]Setting out from Rimmon-perez, they camped at Libnah. [21]Setting out from Libnah, they camped

33:5-15 From Egypt to Sinai

This section of the itinerary corresponds substantially to the itinerary in Exodus 12–19: Rameses to Succoth (Exod 12:37) to Etham (Exod 13:20). Next they encamp at Pi-hahiroth, opposite Baal-zephon, opposite Migdol. As the story is told in the book of Exodus, this is the site of the deliverance at the sea (see Exod 14:2, 9), identified in song and tradition as the Red Sea (Exod 15:4; Deut 11:4; Josh 2:10; 4:23; Ps 136:15). In Numbers 33, however, this sea is unnamed and there is no report of an encounter with Pharaoh's chariots, only that the people crossed over through the sea into the wilderness. The unidentified sea here is probably one of the marshy lakes in the area of today's Suez Canal, around Lake Timsah or the Bitter Lakes. Then between Elim (see Exod 15:27) and the wilderness of Sin (Exod 16:1), the people camp beside the Red Sea. What is probably meant here is the northern tip of the Gulf of Suez. The next two sites are otherwise unknown: Dophkah and Alush. From Alush they move to Rephidim where the people complain about lack of water and where they are attacked by the Amalekites (Exod 17). From Rephidim they go to Sinai.

33:16-36 From Sinai to Kadesh

The first two sites of this section correspond to the narrative in Numbers. At Kibroth-hattaavah the people cried for meat (Num 11:4-15, 18-24, 31-35).

at Rissah. ²²Setting out from Rissah, they camped at Kehelathah. ²³Setting out from Kehelathah, they camped at Mount Shepher. ²⁴Setting out from Mount Shepher, they camped at Haradah. ²⁵Setting out from Haradah, they camped at Makheloth. ²⁶Setting out from Makheloth, they camped at Tahath. ²⁷Setting out from Tahath, they camped at Terah. ²⁸Setting out from Terah, they camped at Mithkah. ²⁹Setting out from Mithkah, they camped at Hashmonah. ³⁰Setting out from Hashmonah, they camped at Moseroth. ³¹Setting out from Moseroth, they camped at Bene-jaakan. ³²Setting out from Bene-jaakan, they camped at Mount Gidgad. ³³Setting out from Mount Gidgad, they camped at Jotbathah. ³⁴Setting out from Jotbathah, they camped at Abronah. ³⁵Setting out from Abronah, they camped at Ezion-geber. ³⁶Setting out from Ezion-geber, they camped in the wilderness of Zin, that is, Kadesh.

From Kadesh to the Plains of Moab. ³⁷Setting out from Kadesh, they camped at Mount Hor on the border of the land of Edom.

³⁸Aaron the priest ascended Mount Hor at the LORD's direction, and there he died in the fortieth year after the departure of the Israelites from the land of Egypt, on the first day of the fifth month. ³⁹Aaron was a hundred and twenty-three years old when he died on Mount Hor.

At Hazeroth Miriam and Aaron complained against Moses (Num 12:1-16). The next seventeen sites are unknown. Ezion-geber, at the head of the Gulf of Aqaba, became a shipping port for Solomon in the tenth century (1 Kgs 9:26). From there the people went to Kadesh in the wilderness of Zin (Num 20:1). The Priestly tradition represented here portrays the people spending most of the forty-year sojourn in the Sinai peninsula and arriving at Kadesh only in the fortieth year (see Num 20:1, 22-29). It was there that the first of the wilderness leaders, Miriam, died. The other tradition represented in these stories has the people arrive at Kadesh much earlier, perhaps little more than a year after the exodus event. From there Moses sends the scouts to reconnoiter the land and there God condemns the exodus generation to wander in the wilderness for forty years until all of them have died except Caleb and Joshua (Num 13–14).

33:37-49 From Kadesh to the Plains of Moab

This section of the itinerary begins with the story of Aaron's death on Mount Hor. New details are added: the year of Aaron's death (the first day of the fifth month in the fortieth year after the exodus) and Aaron's age (123 years). This corresponds to the notice in Exodus 7:7 where Aaron was said to be 83 years old at the time of the exodus. The notice that the king of Arad heard of Israel's approach is probably an allusion to the victory over Arad in 21:1-3.

⁴⁰When the Canaanite, the king of Arad, who ruled over the Negeb in the land of Canaan, heard that the Israelites were coming. . . .

⁴¹Setting out from Mount Hor, they camped at Zalmonah. ⁴²Setting out from Zalmonah, they camped at Punon. ⁴³Setting out from Punon, they camped at Oboth. ⁴⁴Setting out from Oboth, they camped at Iye-abarim on the border of Moab. ⁴⁵Setting out from Iye-abarim, they camped at Dibon-gad. ⁴⁶Setting out from Dibon-gad, they camped at Almon-diblathaim. ⁴⁷Setting out from Almon-diblathaim, they camped in the Abarim range opposite Nebo. ⁴⁸Setting out from the Abarim range, they camped on the plains of Moab by the Jordan opposite Jericho. ⁴⁹They camped by the Jordan on the plains of Moab extended from Beth-jeshimoth to Abel-shittim.

Conquest and Division of Canaan. ⁵⁰The LORD spoke to Moses on the plains of Moab by the Jordan opposite Jericho: ⁵¹Speak to the Israelites and say to them: When you go across the Jordan into the land of Canaan, ⁵²dispossess all the inhabitants of the land before you; destroy all their stone figures, destroy all their molten images, and demolish all their high places.

⁵³You will take possession of the land and settle in it, for I have given you the land to possess. ⁵⁴You will apportion the land among yourselves by lot, clan by clan, assigning a large heritage to a large clan and a small heritage to a small clan. Wherever anyone's lot falls, there will

---

Of the stages between Mount Hor and the plains of Moab, Oboth and Iye-abarim are mentioned elsewhere as camping sites after the incident with the fiery serpents (Num 21:10-12). God sends Moses up the Abarim Mountains to glimpse the Promised Land, which he is not allowed to enter (Num 27:12). From there the people arrive at the plains of Moab where they will encamp until they cross the Jordan under Joshua's leadership (Josh 3).

33:50-56 Conquest and division of Canaan

At this point in the chapter the focus turns to the future. Moses is told to give instructions to the Israelites regarding their entrance into Canaan. They are to be careful to do four things: (1) to drive out all the inhabitants; (2) to destroy all the signs of worship of other gods—carved and molten images as well as high places; (3) to divide the land both by size of clan and by lot (see ch. 26); and (4) to take possession of the land. The current inhabitants will remain a problem if they fail to drive them out and the Lord will begin to treat the Israelites like Canaanites. In other texts the danger of allowing the current inhabitants to remain is the likelihood that Israel will be drawn to worship their gods (Exod 23:24, 33; Deut 7:16). This apostasy will lead to Israel's punishment.

his possession be; you will apportion these shares within your ancestral tribe.

⁵⁵But if you do not dispossess the inhabitants of the land before you, those whom you allow to remain will become barbs in your eyes and thorns in your sides, and they will harass you in the land where you live, ⁵⁶and I will treat you as I had intended to treat them.

34 The Boundaries. ¹The LORD spoke to Moses: ²Give the Israelites this order: When you enter the land of Canaan, this is the territory that shall fall to you as your heritage—the land of Canaan with its boundaries:

³Your southern boundary will be at the wilderness of Zin along the border of Edom; on the east your southern boundary will begin at the end of the

34:1-15 The boundaries

The preparation for entering the Promised Land continues. The land of Canaan is Israel's heritage, in other words, the land promised to Abraham by God. The land east of the Jordan is not included, so only nine and a half tribes will live in what is here considered the Promised Land. The Transjordanian tribes live outside the Promised Land proper.

The boundaries of the land are outlined, beginning in the south. Judah, the major tribe of the south, leads the list of tribal leaders (v. 19), so the southern boundary is the first to be declared. The southern boundary begins at the Dead Sea, bends south as far as Kadesh-Barnea (60–80 miles), and then runs northwest to the Mediterranean Sea south of Gaza. The western boundary is easy to chart: the Mediterranean coastline. The northern boundary begins close to Mount Hor (50–60 miles north of Sidon; not the Mount Hor where Aaron died) and extends about 90 miles east to Hazar-Enan. The eastern boundary runs straight south from there about 125 miles and then runs west to just south of the Sea of Galilee (Chinnereth). From there it extends along the east side of the Jordan River to the Dead Sea. The territory east of the Jordan—the territory given to Reuben, Gad, and half of Manasseh—is not included in Canaan, however, nor is Moab or Edom.

On today's map, the territory would include most of modern Israel and Palestine except the southern tip that extends to Eilat and the Gulf of Aqaba. It also includes a portion of northern Sinai just west of the Gaza strip. On the north it includes most of Lebanon and the western part of Syria.

These boundaries are obviously idealized. The greatest surprise is the extent of territory to the north and east. The territory enclosed by these boundaries was never totally under Israelite control. The boundaries com-

Salt Sea. ⁴Then your boundary will turn south of the Akrabbim Pass and cross Zin. Terminating south of Kadesh-barnea, it extends to Hazar-addar and crosses to Azmon. ⁵Then the boundary will turn from Azmon to the Wadi of Egypt and terminate at the Sea.

⁶For your western boundary you will have the Great Sea with its coast; this will be your western boundary.

⁷This will be your boundary on the north: from the Great Sea you will draw a line to Mount Hor, ⁸and draw it from Mount Hor to Lebo-hamath, with the boundary terminating at Zedad. ⁹Then the boundary extends to Ziphron and terminates at Hazar-enan. This will be your northern boundary.

¹⁰For your eastern boundary you will draw a line from Hazar-enan to Shepham. ¹¹From Shepham the boundary will go down to Riblah, east of Ain, and descending further, the boundary will strike the ridge on the east side of the Sea of Chinnereth; ¹²then the boundary will descend along the Jordan and terminate with the Salt Sea.

This will be your land, with the boundaries that surround it.

¹³Moses also gave this order to the Israelites: "This is the land, to be apportioned among you by lot, which the Lord has commanded to be given to the nine and a half tribes. ¹⁴For the tribe of the Reubenites according to their ancestral houses, and the tribe of the Gadites according to their ancestral houses, as well as half of the tribe of Manasseh, have already received their heritage; ¹⁵these two and a half tribes have received their heritage across the Jordan opposite Jericho, in the east, toward the sunrise."

Supervisors of the Allotment. ¹⁶The Lord spoke to Moses: ¹⁷These are the names of the men who shall apportion the land among you: Eleazar the priest, and Joshua, son of Nun; ¹⁸and you will designate one leader from each of the tribes to apportion the land. ¹⁹These are the names of the men:

---

pare most closely to the Egyptian province of Canaan from the fifteenth to thirteenth centuries B.C. Ezekiel describes the ideal Israel with similar boundaries (47:13–48:29). See map on page 155.

34:16-29 Supervisors of the allotment

The leaders who shall oversee the division of this land among the nine and a half tribes are Eleazar the priest as religious leader and Joshua as civil and military leader. Only ten tribal leaders are named to assist. Reuben and Gad already have their territory and so need no one to represent them in a later division of land. Manasseh, however, is included in order to represent the half of that tribe that will settle west of the Jordan. None of the names correspond to the tribal leaders who assisted Moses in the census of chapter 1. None of the scouts chosen in chapter 13 appear either except Caleb, whose survival is a reward for his fidelity. Otherwise this list represents a new generation.

from the tribe of Judah: Caleb, son of Jephunneh, ²⁰from the tribe of the Simeonites: Samuel, son of Ammihud; ²¹from the tribe of Benjamin: Elidad, son of Chislon; ²²from the tribe of the Danites: a leader, Bukki, son of Jogli; ²³for the descendants of Joseph: from the tribe of the Manassites: a leader, Hanniel, son of Ephod; and ²⁴from the tribe of the Ephraimites: a leader, Kemuel, son of Shiphtan; ²⁵from the tribe of the Zebulunites: a leader, Elizaphan, son of Parnach; ²⁶from the tribe of the Issacharites: a leader, Paltiel, son of Azzan;

²⁷from the tribe of the Asherites: a leader, Ahihud, son of Shelomi; ²⁸from the tribe of the Naphtalites: a leader, Pedahel, son of Ammihud.

²⁹These are the ones whom the LORD commanded to apportion to the Israelites their heritage in the land of Canaan.

35 **Cities for the Levites.** ¹The LORD spoke to Moses on the plains of Moab by the Jordan opposite Jericho: ²Command the Israelites out of the heritage they possess to give the Levites cities to dwell in; you will also give the Levites the pasture lands around the cities. ³The cities will be for them to dwell in, and the pasture lands will be for their cattle, their flocks, and all their other ani-

35:1-8 Cities for the Levites

The Levites have been treated separately from the rest of the Israelites throughout this book. They were omitted from the original census (1:47-54; 2:33) and counted as substitutes for the firstborn (3:5-16, 40-50). They were numbered again (4:34-49) and purified for service to the sanctuary (8:5-26; see 18:2-6). They are granted special tithes and obligated to pay tithes in turn (18:21-32; see 31:30, 47). When the second census was taken for the purpose of apportioning the land, the Levites were again omitted and then numbered separately (26:57-62) because the Levites have no share in the inheritance of the land (18:23-24; see Deut 10:8-9; 14:27-29; 18:1-2).

Therefore another arrangement has to be made for the Levites, since they will not share in the division of land. They are to be given cities with pastureland by each of the other tribes, more from the larger tribes and fewer from the smaller tribes. (The number of cities assigned for each tribe to donate is set and the cities named in Josh 21.) The measurements of these grants are unclear, but apparently the cities are to be 2,000 cubits square and the pasturelands extend outward from the city walls for another 1,000 cubits. Thus the whole plot would be 4,000 cubits square. The total number of cities is to be forty-eight, six of which are to be cities of asylum.

mals. ⁴The pasture lands of the cities to be assigned the Levites shall extend a thousand cubits out from the city walls in every direction. ⁵You will measure out two thousand cubits outside the city along the east side, two thousand cubits along the south side, two thousand cubits along the west side, and two thousand cubits along the north side, with the city lying in the center. These will be the pasture lands of their cities.

⁶Now these are the cities you will give to the Levites: the six cities of asylum which you must establish for the homicide to run to, and in addition forty-two other cities—⁷a total of forty-eight cities with their pasture lands which you will assign to the Levites. ⁸In assigning the cities from what the Isra-elites possess, take more from a larger group and fewer from a smaller one, so that each will cede cities to the Levites in proportion to the heritage which it receives.

Cities of Asylum. ⁹The LORD spoke to Moses: ¹⁰Speak to the Israelites and say to them: When you go across the Jordan into the land of Canaan, ¹¹select for yourselves cities to serve as cities of asylum, where a homicide who has killed someone inadvertently may flee. ¹²These cities will serve you as places of asylum from the avenger of blood, so that a homicide will not be put to death until tried before the community. ¹³As for the cities you assign, you will have six cities of asylum: ¹⁴you will designate three cities beyond the Jordan, and you

35:9-15 Cities of asylum

The cities of asylum are places of refuge where a killer may flee until it is determined whether he is guilty of murder or manslaughter. (The cities are further described and named in Josh 20; see also Deut 19:1-13.) This place of refuge is necessary because, without it, the next-of-kin might avenge the killing before a reasoned judgment can take place. The next-of-kin (Hebrew *goʾel*, often translated "redeemer" or "restorer" but here as "avenger"; 35:12, 19, 21, 24, 25, 27; see Josh 20:3, 5, 9) has the responsibility to ransom a relative who is enslaved (Lev 25:48-49), to redeem land that has been lost due to debt (Lev 25:25; see Num 5:8), and to avenge the relative's murder. These cities of asylum must be spaced so that it is possible for a fugitive to reach one before the next-of-kin catches up.

Traditionally sacred places have been considered places of safety for fugitives (see 1 Kgs 1:50-51). Some of the cities named as cities of asylum may have a reputation as sacred sites: Shechem was the site of a temple to Baal Berith; the name of Kedesh is based on the word for "holy" (*qadosh*). Perhaps their reputation as sacred places is the reason for their designation. This association with sacredness may also be the reason that the term of an offender's confinement in the city of asylum is linked to the life of the current high priest.

will designate three cities in the land of Canaan. These will be cities of asylum. [15]These six cities will serve as places of asylum for the Israelites, and for the resident or transient aliens among them, so that anyone who has killed a person inadvertently may flee there.

Murder and Manslaughter. [16]If someone strikes another with an iron instrument and causes death, that person is a murderer, and the murderer must be put to death. [17]If someone strikes another with a death-dealing stone in the hand and death results, that person is a murderer, and the murderer must be put to death. [18]Or if someone strikes another with a death-dealing club in the hand and death results, that person is a murderer, and the murderer must be put to death. [19]The avenger of blood is the one who will kill the murderer, putting the individual to death on sight.

[20]If someone pushes another out of hatred, or throws something from an ambush, and death results, [21]or strikes another with the hand out of enmity and death results, the assailant must be put to death as a murderer. The avenger of blood will kill the murderer on sight.

[22]However, if someone pushes another without malice aforethought, or without lying in ambush throws some object at another, [23]or without seeing drops upon another some death-dealing stone and death results, although there was neither enmity nor malice—[24]then the community will judge between the assailant and the avenger of blood in accordance with these norms. [25]The community will deliver the homicide from the avenger of blood and the community will return the homicide to the city of asylum where the latter had fled; and the individual will stay there until the death of the high priest who has been anointed with sacred oil. [26]If the homicide leaves at all the bounds of the city of asylum to which flight had been made, [27]and is found by the avenger of blood beyond the bounds of the city of asylum, and the avenger of blood kills the homicide, the avenger incurs no bloodguilt; [28]for the

---

35:16-30 Murder and manslaughter

Several examples are given for distinguishing between premeditated murder and manslaughter. If someone kills another deliberately with a weapon or if the one who kills another hates the victim and has planned the killing, that person is a murderer and must be put to death. The *go'el* is designated as the executioner. If the death is accidental, however, and there is no history of conflict between the two, then there is no cause for the death penalty. The one who caused the death is to be taken back from the place of judgment to the city of asylum and must remain there until the death of the high priest. After the death of the high priest, the one who killed accidentally may return to home in safety. If the killer leaves the city of asylum before the death of the high priest, however, the *go'el* may execute that person without penalty.

homicide was required to stay in the city of asylum until the death of the high priest. Only after the death of the high priest may the homicide return to the land of the homicide's possession.

²⁹This is the statute for you throughout all your generations, wherever you live, for rendering judgment.

Judgment. ³⁰Whenever someone kills another, the evidence of witnesses is required to kill the murderer. A single witness does not suffice for putting a person to death.

No Indemnity. ³¹You will not accept compensation in place of the life of a murderer who deserves to die, but that person must be put to death. ³²Nor will you accept compensation to allow one who has fled to a city of asylum to return to live in the land before the death of the high priest. ³³You will not pollute the land where you live. For bloodshed pollutes the land, and the land can have no expiation for the blood shed on it except through the blood of the one who shed it. ³⁴Do not defile the land in which you live and in the midst of which I dwell; for I the LORD dwell in the midst of the Israelites.

36 Inheritance of Daughters. ¹The heads of the ancestral houses in a clan of the descendants of Gilead, son of Machir, son of Manasseh—one of the Josephite clans—came up and spoke

35:30 Judgment

The testimony of at least two witnesses is necessary to convict someone of a capital crime and to execute that person (see Deut 17:6). Deuteronomy expands this law: No one may be convicted of any crime without the testimony of two or three witnesses (Deut 19:15).

35:31-34 No indemnity

A person who is subject to the death penalty cannot be rescued by either a ransom or a bribe. Nor can one who is confined to a city of asylum buy freedom before the death of the high priest. These legal decisions are final and must be carried out in full.

This legislation is based on the principle that life is sacred and bloodshed pollutes the land. In the story of the first murder, God says to Cain, "Your brother's blood cries out to me from the ground!" (Gen 4:10). The pollution must be removed, because of God's presence in the land. The understanding in these laws is that the only thing that can cleanse the land from this pollution is the blood of the perpetrator. Blood is the sign of life; blood cleanses blood.

36:1-11 Inheritance of daughters

The daughters of Zelophehad have been given the right to take possession of their father's share of the Promised Land since he died with no sons (see 27:1-11). The men from the same clan as Zelophehad now raise before Moses and Eleazar the priest and before the leaders who were the heads of the ancestral houses of the Israelites. ²They said: "The LORD commanded my lord to apportion the land by lot for a heritage among the Israelites; and my lord was commanded by the LORD to give the heritage of Zelophehad our kinsman to his daughters. ³But if they marry into one of the other Israelite tribes, their heritage will be withdrawn from our ancestral heritage and will be added to that of the tribe into which they marry; thus the heritage that fell to us by lot will be diminished. ⁴When the Israelites celebrate the jubilee year, the heritage of these women will be added to that of the tribe into which they marry and their heritage will be withdrawn from that of our ancestral tribe."

⁵So Moses commanded the Israelites at the direction of the LORD: "The tribe of the Josephites are right in what they say. ⁶This is what the LORD commands with regard to the daughters of Zelophehad: They may marry anyone they please, provided they marry into a clan of their ancestral tribe, ⁷so that no heritage of the Israelites will pass from one tribe to another, but all the Israelites will retain their own ancestral heritage. ⁸Every daughter who inherits property in

---

a concern. They speak to the same group that the daughters addressed: Moses, Eleazar the priest, and the tribal leaders. They recognize that the right given to the daughters of Zelophehad was commanded by the Lord. But they point out that this may lead to a diminishment of the land allotted to the tribe of Manasseh.

According to custom, the land owned by these women will be inherited by their sons. But sons are counted as members not of their mother's but of their father's tribe. If the daughters of Zelophehad marry men from another tribe than Manasseh, the land will transfer to that tribe. Not even the jubilee will solve this difficulty. At the jubilee land that has been sold or lost because of debt is returned to the original tribe (Lev 25:13-17, 23-28), but the jubilee does not apply to land that transfers because of inheritance. Thus, although the daughters of Zelophehad have ensured that their father's heritage will not be lost in their generation, it may be lost in the next generation.

Moses resolves the difficulty by issuing a new command, restricting the rights of daughters who inherit the family property. Because the land of any tribe should not be lost, these women must marry within their ancestral tribe. The daughters of Zelophehad, therefore, must marry someone from the tribe of Manasseh. Tribal rights to the land supersede women's rights. The daughters of Zelophehad obey the command by marrying their first cousins. Because of them two laws have been initiated: the right of daughters to inherit if they have no brothers and the obligation of the same daughters to marry within their own tribe.

any of the Israelite tribes will marry someone belonging to a clan of her own ancestral tribe, in order that all the Israelites may remain in possession of their own ancestral heritage. ⁹Thus, no heritage will pass from one tribe to another, but all the Israelite tribes will retain their own ancestral heritage."

¹⁰The daughters of Zelophehad did exactly as the LORD commanded Moses. ¹¹Mahlah, Tirzah, Hoglah, Milcah and Noah, Zelophehad's daughters, married sons of their uncles on their father's side. ¹²They married within the clans of the descendants of Manasseh, son of Joseph; hence their heritage remained in the tribe of their father's clan.

Conclusion. ¹³These are the commandments and decisions which the LORD commanded the Israelites through Moses, on the plains of Moab beside the Jordan opposite Jericho.

36:13 Conclusion

The book of Numbers concludes with the statement that the prescriptions in this book were commanded by the Lord and announced to the Israelites through Moses. The statement that what is being promulgated is what the Lord has commanded Moses appears several times (33x) throughout Numbers (1:19, 54; 2:33, 34; 3:16, 42, 51; 4:49; 8:3, 20, 22; 9:5; 15:22-23, 36; 17:26; 20:9, 27; 26:4; 27:11, 22, 23; 30:1, 2, 17; 31:7, 21, 31, 41, 47; 34:13; 36:5, 10). The same declaration is made at the end of Exodus (40:16, 19, 21, 23, 25, 27, 29, 32), Leviticus (27:34), and Deuteronomy (34:9-12). In Exodus and Leviticus Israel is still at Sinai. In Numbers and Deuteronomy Israel is on the plains of Moab, poised to cross the Jordan into the Promised Land.

REVIEW AIDS AND DISCUSSION TOPICS

Introduction *(pages 5–10)*

1. What do both the English and the Hebrew titles of this book tell us about its contents?

2. When (chronologically) and where (geographically) do the stories in Numbers take place?

3. What is the difference between the "Priestly" and the "pre-Priestly" traditions in Numbers?

4. How is the wilderness theme both a positive and a negative symbol in the Old Testament?

5. Name and discuss the five insights to be gained from a thoughtful study of this book.

1:1–10:10 Census and preparation for the departure from Sinai *(pages 11–46)*

1. Why is the census total of 603,550 an unrealistic number? What meanings might this number have?

2. Why are the Levites excluded from the census? What are the duties of the Levites?

3. What three groups are expelled and why?

4. Describe and discuss such elements as the ordeal for suspected adultery, the Nazirite laws, the priestly blessing, the purification of the Levites, and the second Passover.

10:11–25:18 Departure, rebellion, and wandering in the wilderness for forty years *(pages 46–109)*

1. What should be said about the obvious contradictions in the text so they do not disturb the reader?

2. Describe and discuss such incidents as the following: the appearance of quail; the jealousy of Aaron and Mariam; Miriam's leprosy and why she is punished and not Aaron; Moses' arguments with the Lord to reverse punishment; the rebellions of Dathan, Abiram, and Korah and their punishment.

3. Describe and discuss such incidents as the ashes of the red heifer (why red?) and the use of the ashes, the sin of Moses and Aaron, the deaths of Miriam and Aaron.

4. Describe the incident of the bronze serpent and explain its connection with John 3:14-15.

5. Review the stories about the seer Balaam in chapters 22–24, with special attention to the fable of the talking donkey and the connection between the fourth oracle (24:14-25) and the story of the magi and the star of Bethlehem in Matthew 2.

26:1–36:13 Second census of a new generation, preparation to enter the Promised Land *(pages 109–149)*

1. What are the two purposes for the second census? What are the differences between the first and second censuses?

2. Describe the role played by the daughters of Zelophehad and the change in the law of inheritance.

3. What do you make of the fact that only 6 to 8 percent of the persons given names in the whole Bible are women?

4. Describe the transfer of civil leadership from Moses to his successor in chapter 27.

5. Describe the celebration of the Jewish feasts of Sabbath, New Moon, Passover, Unleavened Bread, Weeks or Pentecost, New Year's, Day of Atonement, and Booths.

6. What are the two purposes of the story of the campaign against the Midianites?

7. Describe the request of the tribes of Gad and Reuben and its significance.

8. Name the four things the Israelites are to do when they enter the land of Canaan.

9. What is the purpose of the cities of asylum and the role of the next-of-kin (Hebrew *go'el*)?

10. Discuss your overall evaluation and reaction to the book of Numbers.

INDEX OF CITATIONS FROM THE
CATECHISM OF THE CATHOLIC CHURCH

The arabic number(s) following the citation refer(s) to the paragraph number(s) in the *Catechism of the Catholic Church*. The asterisk following a paragraph number indicates that the citation has been paraphrased.

Numbers

1:48-53	1539*	12:13-14	2577*
7:89	433*	21:4-9	2130*
11:24-25	1541*	24:17-19	528*
12:3	2576	24:17	528*
12:7-8	2576	28:9	582*

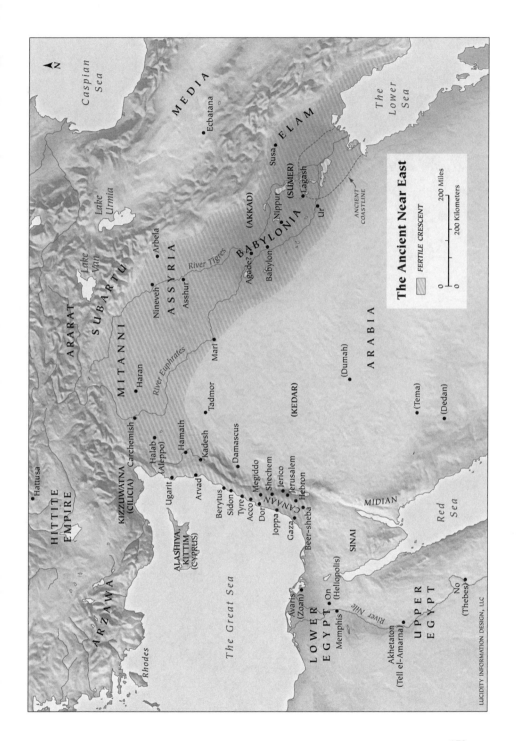

The Ancient Near East

FERTILE CRESCENT

| 0 | 200 Miles |
| 0 | 200 Kilometers |

LUCIDITY INFORMATION DESIGN, LLC

Caspian Sea

MEDIA

Ecbatana

Lake Urmia

Lake Van

ARARAT

SUBARTU

MITANNI

ASSYRIA

Arbela

Nineveh

Asshur

Haran

Mari

River Tigris

River Euphrates

ELAM

Susa

SUMER

Nippur

Lagash

Ur

BABYLONIA

AKKAD

Agade?

Babylon

ANCIENT COASTLINE

The Lower Sea

ARABIA

(Dumah)

(Tema)

(Dedan)

(KEDAR)

Tadmor

Carchemish

Halab (Aleppo)

Hamath

Kadesh

Damascus

Megiddo

Shechem

Jerico

Jerusalem

Hebron

CANAAN

Berytus

Sidon

Tyre

Acco

Dor

Joppa

Gaza

Beer-sheba

Ugarit

Arvad

ALASHIYA, KITTIM (CYPRUS)

HITTITE EMPIRE

Hattusa

KIZZUWATNA (CILICIA)

ARZAWA

Rhodes

The Great Sea

MIDIAN

SINAI

Red Sea

On (Heliopolis)

Avaris (Zoan)

LOWER EGYPT

Memphis

Akhetaton (Tell el-Amarna)

River Nile

UPPER EGYPT

No (Thebes)

N

153

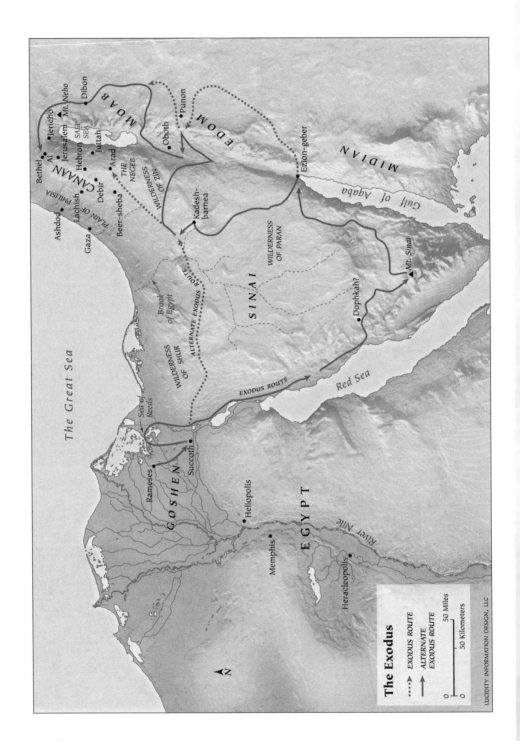

The Exodus

···> EXODUS ROUTE
→ ALTERNATE
   EXODUS ROUTE

| 0 | 50 Miles |
| 0 | 50 Kilometers |

LUCIDITY INFORMATION DESIGN, LLC

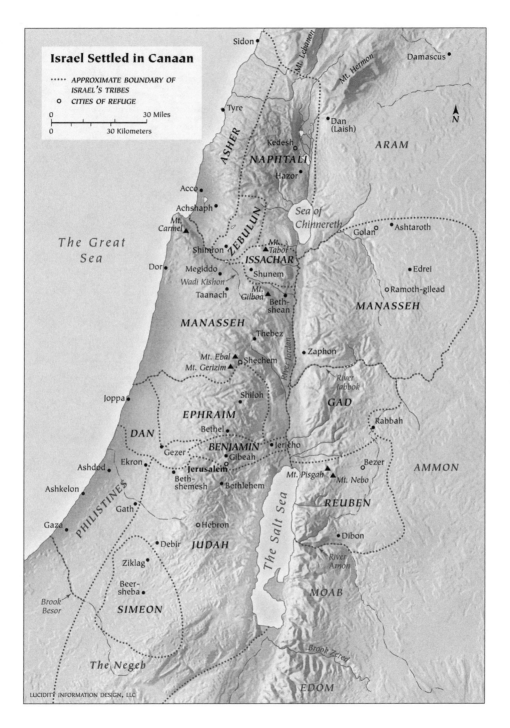

Israel Settled in Canaan

····· APPROXIMATE BOUNDARY OF
ISRAEL'S TRIBES
○ CITIES OF REFUGE

0   30 Miles
0   30 Kilometers

N

Sidon •

Damascus •

Mt. Lebanon

Mt. Hermon

Tyre •

Dan
(Laish) •

ASHER

Kedesh
○

ARAM

NAPHTALI

Hazor •

Acco •

Achshaph •

Mt.
Carmel ▲

ZEBULUN

Sea of
Chinnereth

Golan ○

Ashtaroth •

The Great
Sea

Shimron •

Mt.
▲ Tabor

ISSACHAR

Dor •

Megiddo •

Shunem •

Edrei •

Wadi Kishon

Mt.
Gilboa ▲

Ramoth-gilead ○

Taanach •

Beth-
shean

MANASSEH

MANASSEH

Thebez •

Zaphon •

Mt. Ebal ▲
Mt. Gerizim ▲

○ Shechem

River Jordan

River
Jabbok

Joppa •

Shiloh •

GAD

EPHRAIM

Bethel •

Rabbah •

DAN

Gezer •

BENJAMIN

• Jericho

Ekron •

Gibeah •

Bezer
○

AMMON

Ashdod •

Jerusalem •

Mt. Pisgah ▲

▲ Mt. Nebo

Ashkelon •

Beth-
shemesh •

• Bethlehem

REUBEN

Gath •

The Salt Sea

Gaza •

PHILISTINES

○ Hebron

• Dibon

• Debir

JUDAH

River
Arnon

Ziklag •

Beer-
sheba •

MOAB

Brook
Besor

SIMEON

The Negeb

Brook Zered

LUCIDITY INFORMATION DESIGN, LLC

EDOM

155